101
fun things
to do with
your dog

Alison Smith

hamlyn

An Hachette UK Company
www.hachette.co.uk

First published in Great Britain in 2011 by
Hamlyn, a division of Octopus Publishing Group Ltd
Endeavour House
189 Shaftesbury Avenue
London
WC2H 8JY
www.octopusbooks.co.uk

Alison Smith asserts the moral right to be identified as the author of this work

ISBN 978-0-600-62057-0

A CIP catalogue record for this book is available from the British Library

Printed and bound in China

10 9 8 7 6 5 4 3 2 1

The advice in this book is provided as general information only. It is not necessarily specific to
any individual case and is not a substitute for the guidance and advice provided by a licensed
veterinary practitioner consulted in any particular situation. Octopus Publishing Group
accepts no liability or responsibility for any consequences resulting from the use of or reliance
upon the information contained herein.

No dogs or puppies were harmed in the making of this book.

Dogs are referred to throughout this book as 'he'. The information is equally applicable to
both male and female dogs, unless otherwise specified.

Contents

Introduction

Being active and playing games with your dog is good for his physical and mental wellbeing – as well as your own. We all know the joys that owning a dog can bring: walks in the park, runs on the beach and games of catch are just some of the activities you can enjoy with your four-legged friend. But it doesn't have to end there – in fact, we've found 101 fantastic ways to have fun with your dog. Enjoying different activities and games together will not only add more to your days out (or days in!), but will also result in a very well-trained and happy dog into the bargain.

In this book, we give you plenty of ideas to turn an ordinary walk into an interactive and enjoyable afternoon, and tell you how you can turn even the laziest Labrador or the most reluctant Rottweiler into

a dog that will bring you his lead and ask you to take him out to play. None of the activities require you to have dazzling dog-training skills, although some basic training will help; they are all simple games that need a little patience and a small amount of time.

We have included some of the canine disciplines that offer you and your dog an opportunity to become proficient in a number of sports. You may even hit on an activity that offers the chance to enter competitions and compete against other owners and their dogs.

HAVE FUN WITH TRAINING

You can dip in and out of the book and choose any of the games and activities, but it's advisable to start with those in the first chapter, Training Games. It will be much easier to get your dog to participate and learn new skills if he has first undergone some basic training. Making training into a game is a very positive way for your dog to learn and will be fun for both of you.

All the activities in this book use praise and positive actions or rewards, rather than punishment, to teach your dog new skills and good behaviour – an approach known as positive reinforcement. To train your dog in this way you simply need to work out what motivates him – usually it's the promise of a tasty treat or his favourite toy, or even just physical affection and praise – and use that motivator as a reward when he behaves in the correct way. Do your

Clicker training

In some of the games, we've recommended using a training device called a clicker, which enables you to respond fast and accurately to your dog's positive behaviour. You simply press the clicker when your dog does as you ask and he understands that the 'click' means he's behaved in the right way – and pleased you – and that a reward (a tasty treat or his favourite toy) will follow. When he hears the click, he will associate it with his most recent good behaviour and anticipate the reward. Timing the click correctly is crucial:

1 You give the command – for example, sit. It's best to use a hand signal as well as a specific word.

2 Your dog obeys your command and sits.

3 As soon as his bottom touches the floor, you press the clicker.

4 The dog hears the click, realises he has done well and awaits his reward. It's important to reward him immediately so that he associates receiving the treat with the good behaviour.

best to ignore bad behaviour, in the same way you might with a small child. If you respond to unwanted behaviour, your dog may enjoy the attention or simply get confused and behave badly again. Shouting at, coercing or physically punishing a dog are ineffective ways to train him – such methods simply cause your dog to be confused and fearful and may even result in him responding to aggression with aggression.

You'll soon learn what best motivates your dog, but food treats are bound to be on his list of favourite things. Make sure the treat is tasty, has a strong smell, and is easy for your dog to eat – he has to be able to swallow it in a matter of seconds for it to be effective in training. Pieces of chicken, smoked

Key to the symbols

 Number of dogs needed

 Number of people needed

 Outdoor activity

 Indoor activity

 Outdoor or indoor activity

ham, sausage and cheese are all good choices. With all treat-giving games, make sure that you adjust your dog's meals accordingly if he's eaten a lot of treats.

To begin with, you will need to reward your dog every time he does as he is asked. Once he has mastered a skill, though, such as lying down or staying, he will respond immediately that he sees or hears the cue and it won't be necessary to reward him every time. Do, however, always try to praise him because his main aim will be to please you.

A final word about training: be patient, consistent and persistent. You will both get there in the end and hopefully have some fun along the way.

A BOOK FOR ALL DOGS

It does not matter whether you have a prize pedigree dog or an aged crossbreed – the saying 'You can't teach an old dog new tricks' does not apply to the following pages. Indeed, many of my dogs have enjoyed a new lease of life after being taught some motivational games to beat boredom and get their old bones on the move again.

Some of the games and activities in this book are designed for just one dog/one person, whereas others are for more than one dog and more than one person. In many cases, you will need some props or specific items, and don't forget the treats.

So, get that collar and lead ready...and let's go! Have fun!

Some things to remember

- Before you begin to play games, make sure you can easily take things away from your dog.

- Don't play rough and tumble wrestling games or allow your dog to chase children. Both are exciting for your dog but can encourage games that are out of your control.

- Have frequent, daily, play sessions at home and when out for walks.

- Play in short bursts of up to 15 minutes (depending on the pace of the game) and finish while your dog still wants to play.

- When playing, use an exciting voice with lots of praise and encouragement.

- When a dog is keen to play, only start the game when he is doing something you want, such as lying down quietly. This will encourage good behaviour.

- Tidy toys away at the end of each play session (with help from your dog, if you wish).

- Never force your dog to play if he does not want to.

Training Games

Generally speaking, all dogs have the same understanding and ability to learn, and they will be better dogs – and you will be a better owner – for taking advantage of this. Without any basic training, a dog may be a wonderful companion and friend for you, but how do you know that he is safe and reliable in all situations? The answer is that you don't. However, by doing some fun dog training every few days, you can give yourself and your dog the opportunity to learn together and bond. You don't need to be a professional dog trainer to achieve this; some simple games and regular playtime together will work wonders. All in all, dog-training games are a great way to stimulate your dog both physically and mentally. They are useful training methods to help develop his confidence, prevent undesirable habits, alleviate boredom and acquire useful skills. Two good props you might want to consider purchasing are a clicker (see page 5) – available in pet stores and from the internet – and a whistle, which will save your voice!

To get your dog to sit, arm yourself with some treats (and a clicker if you are using one). Make sure there is nothing going on around you that will distract him. With your dog on the lead, face him and say 'Sit', using your clicker (if you use one) at the same time as you give the command. Obviously he will wonder what on earth you are saying, so repeat it, this time pushing gently on his bottom until his back legs lower. Give him a treat when he gets it right and never use unnecessary force. The aim with this simple command is to repeat it often (and over a few days), until he does it on his own using only your command.

Once you have mastered the sit, move on to teaching him stay. Again, the aim here is repetition of the command (using treats and a clicker), to get your dog to stay for longer periods of time and to allow you to walk away from him until you are ready for him to move. It's better if you can get him to sit first. Then, on the command 'Stay', move away from him slowly – just a couple of steps at first. If he looks like he wants to move, repeat the command 'Stay'. Once you have allowed a bit of space between you, approach him and treat him. As with the sit, this may take a few days for him to learn. But it's well within your reach, even with an older dog.

Or try this: Rather than pushing down gently on your dog's hindquarters when you teach him to sit, hold a treat in your hand just above his nose. Move it upwards and backwards. As your dog's head goes up to follow the treat, his bottom will automatically do down onto the ground in a sitting position.

Sit and Stay

We'll leave the roll over until later!

You'll also need: a collar and lead, treats, a clicker (optional)

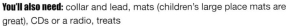

You'll also need: collar and lead, mats (children's large place mats are great), CDs or a radio, treats

Musical Chairs

Test your dog's sit and stay

This is exactly as its name suggests: a game of 'musical chairs' for a dog.

Start by placing the mats – how many you use is up to you – in a circle or a line. Attach a lead to your dog's collar and ask a friend to start the music. Walk your dog around – or up and down – the mats until the music stops. As soon as it does, ask your dog to 'Sit' on the mat nearest to him. Use the 'Stay' command until the music starts up again. Reward him with a treat at the end of each sit and stay.

Some dogs quickly pick up on the fact that the music stopping means sit, whereas others take a while longer. Even if you never get that far, it's still a fun game for both of you.

Or try this: Why not involve the children? Ask them to put some chairs out and join in. You can alternate the chairs with the mats if you wish. You or one of the children can handle the dog on a lead to stop him getting over-excited or confused.

To begin, ask your dog to sit in front of you. Kneel down and hold a treat in your hand near to his nose. Use a treat and slowly lower it towards the ground, keeping it very close to his nose. Praise him constantly all the while his body is moving into the down position. As he follows the treat with his nose, his front legs will go down automatically until his elbows touch the ground and the rest of his body will follow. As soon as he drops down, click (if using)

and praise. This way he will know that he is doing the correct thing. Give him the treat when he is on the floor. Gradually introduce the word 'Down', but only when he is in the down position.

If, at any point he tries to raise himself, use the treat and the command 'Down' straight away to get him back to where you want him. Again, use the clicker if you wish. Praise him as soon as he starts to go back down again.

Repeat this process about five times per training session, always using praise and treats as positive reassurance. You can practise this anywhere and everywhere, which will help your dog to associate the act with the command, and not with the fact that he's in a certain place at a specific time.

Or try this: If your dog becomes silly during this activity – he may decide to roll over or flop onto his side – don't become impatient. Stop the game and try again another time. Never attempt a training game such as this one if you think that your dog is getting bored as it will not work.

Down, Boy!

A simple game with valuable results

3

You'll also need: treats, a clicker (optional)

You'll also need: treats

Watch Me

Get your dog's undivided attention

Teaching your dog to pay attention to you is very important. If you can get him to ignore things around him and focus exclusively on you, it will be much easier to teach him things. You should never stare into your a dog's eyes. Dogs interpret staring as a challenge and some may even become aggressive, although this only happens in very isolated cases. Looking into your dog's eyes for a moment or two is fine, but stop if he begins to look uncomfortable.

Conceal some of your dog's favourite treats in your pocket or hand. Now face him and, as soon as he looks right at you, say, 'Watch me'. Immediately give him a treat and praise him.

You will find that your dog watches you most of the time naturally. The next time you pick up his food bowl or lead and he is watching you, simply say 'Watch' and gradually he will learn what the command means. Practise this every time he is watching you. It may take a while before your dog understands, but when you think he knows the command 'Watch me' try the game again. If he doesn't look at you, don't say anything – just try again another time. Praise him whenever he does what he is supposed to do.

Or try this: To get your dog's attention, hold the treat up to your eye briefly. His eyes will almost certainly follow it.

First, remember that you are the boss. You make the rules, and that means that your dog should not drag you into the car behind him, nor dangerously bolt out of the car the minute you stop and open the door.

Decide where you want your dog to travel in the car. In the back is safer, especially if you have a station wagon or 4x4. Walk your dog to the car on the lead and put him in a sit. Open the car door and then give the wait . If he tries to pull forward, calmly put him back in to a sit and start again.

When you are ready, say 'Go' and encourage your dog to get into the car. Reward him immediately with a treat if he does this without pulling. Repeat this as often as necessary – eventually, you will be able to take off his lead while he waits patiently for the command to get in.

Getting out safely requires the same diligence. Attach the lead to your dog's collar in the car and tell him to 'Wait'. On the command 'Go', he should get out of the car sensibly and without getting over-excited or trying to run away and play. Again, reward his good behaviour with a tasty treat.

This is a good routine to practise and get right before you visit new places. That way you will have a well-mannered and reliable travelling companion.

Or try this: You don't have to restrict this to a car. You can teach your dog to allow you to go through doors before him, or wait until you tell him to come into the house after a walk. Remember that all these 'training' games are fun for your dog and he will enjoy trying to please you.

After You

Car etiquette for dogs

You'll also need: a collar and lead, treats

You'll also need: a collar and lead, treats

Meet and Greet

How to have a polite pooch

You will most certainly impress people if you have a well-mannered dog, both when you are out and about or when you have visitors at home.

Ideally, a puppy needs to meet at least three new people every day, so you must maintain a social life at home or walk your dog regularly – even an adult dog will benefit from meeting different people. When around people (and other dogs), always keep your dog on the lead until you are confident that he knows how to greet people properly.

You can also encourage people to greet your dog while he is on the lead. Praise him when he allows people to pet him and reward him with a treat for his good behaviour. Do not encourage him to jump up at them. If he tries to do so, firmly use the command 'No', and gently pull him back. As he gets to know the rules – and when you feel comfortable – you can allow people to approach him off the lead and make a fuss of him.

Or try this: Invite some children round and let your dog interact with them. Show the children how to make him sit, especially as they may want to encourage your dog to jump up. Again, use praise and rewards for good and gentle behaviour. This will give him – and you – reassurance about how he will react with others when he is out and about.

This is an important training game, of which your dog will never tire. Get a family member or friend to kneel down and hold your dog gently by his collar. You kneel about 3 m (10 ft) away and call your dog by his name (use the clicker if wished). When he comes to you, take hold of his collar, make a fuss of him and give him a treat.

If this goes well, it is now your turn to hold him while your friend calls him. Do not let go of the collar until the other person calls, and then release him immediately if he is straining to go.

Keep the sessions short and fun but play this game at least three or four times a week. Eventually the recall game can turn into hide-and-seek. At that point, you can add other people, each with a bag of treats, but make sure they don't all call at once.

This game is one of the best ways to train a young puppy to come to you on command.

Or try this: If your dog is fed dried food, you can play this game at dinner time. Simply divide some of his food amongst yourselves and recall your dog until it has all gone.

The Recall Game

Play ping-pong with your dog!

You'll also need: a collar and lead, treats, a clicker (optional)

You'll also need: treats

Play Dead

A cool game that uses the down command to great effect!

Ask your dog to sit and reward him when he does so. Next, use the 'Down' command while pretending to shoot him. Point your fingers at him and say 'Bang', using a treat to lure him into a lying-down position. Holding a treat, move it in a circular motion near to his head to try to get him to roll onto his back, as if dead. If he does this, give him a treat immediately and lots of verbal praise.

This game does require patience, as you now have to spend time teaching your dog that when you say

'Bang' and point your 'gun' at him, he needs to lie down and roll over on the same command. Eventually he will learn, but never do more than 10 repetitions at a time or he will become bored. The key is to reward him each time he makes even the slightest move you require of him. Sufficient practice will see him drop as you shoot him and roll on to his back with legs splayed and play dead.

Or try this: Use the first 'Bang' to get your dog down and the second 'Bang' to make him roll over.

This game teaches your dog to touch different objects with his nose, using strong-smelling treats as the motivation.

Start by sitting in front of your dog, holding a treat in your hand. Spread out your other hand in front of his nose. The minute his nose touches the centre of your palm, click (if using, to reinforce the command) and give the treat as a reward. If your dog doesn't show any interest in touching your palm, rub a bit of the treat on the centre of it and try again. Repeat this time saying, 'Touch' just before your dog's nose touches your palm. Keep the treats hidden in your other hand, so that you are rewarding your dog for touching your palm and not just feeding him treats.

Or try this: To transfer touch to another object, shape your dog's behaviour by rewarding him for any movement towards an object of your choice. For example, place a ball on the floor a few metres away from your dog. Wait for him to go over to the ball to investigate, then click and treat. If he is not interested in the ball, place a small food treat on it as a lure. Click and say 'Touch' as soon as he reaches the ball; the lure will be his treat. After a few repetitions, try it without the treat. Once confident, move the object away,

perhaps placing it on a chair or a step. The command 'Touch' should be pretty much in place by now.

The Touch Game

Teaching your hound to nose around

You'll also need: cooked sausage pieces (or other tasty treats), a clicker (optional)

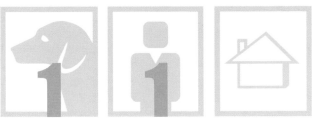

You'll also need: a small bell, treats, a clicker (optional)

Ring My Bell

Teach your dog to ask to go outside

When your dog is reliably touching objects on cue, try the bell game. Hold the bell in your palm and say 'Touch', then as soon as your dog touches the bell, click (if using) and treat. Repeat this step a few times. If your dog is hesitant about touching the bell, smear it with something he likes to eat. Once he is consistently tapping the bell in your hand, set it on the floor. Click and treat when he makes contact with it, gradually introducing the word 'Touch'.

In the next step, when he has become used to the sound, hang the bell up a short distance away from your dog's nose. Repeat the 'Touch' command and treat him when he does as you ask. Once your dog is responding to the word 'Touch' consistently, hang the bell on the doorknob. You may now use going outdoors as the reward for touching the bell.

This game is particularly good for younger dogs, as they will start to associate ringing the bell with being let outside to do their business.

Or try this: The touch game can be altered to take in almost any object, and with a little practice, you can ask your dog to touch most objects. As with the games where he learns to recognize objects and people's names, so too can he be told to go and touch different things with his nose. If you like, you could use the command 'Ring the Bell' instead of 'Touch'. Remember that this is a game to your dog and is all about pleasing you.

In this simple game, fetch is used to entertain your dog. One of the basic training methods is to use two identical toys, which your dog enjoys playing with, in a bait-and-switch routine.

To begin, your dog should be on a lead. Hide one of the toys on your person, then show him the identical one before throwing it a short distance. Release him from the lead and say 'Fetch'. Your dog will chase after the toy and, hopefully, pick it up. When he starts to return with the first toy, click (if using) and reward by giving him the hidden toy. He will probably drop the toy he is carrying in favour of the new one. Wait for him to return to you and then re-attach his lead before throwing the new toy. After throwing it, say 'Fetch' and release your dog to give chase. While he is chasing the new toy, run and retrieve the first one. Repeat this process several times, using the 'Fetch' command.

Or try this: A good tip when playing this game is to hold your dog for a moment before releasing him to chase the object. This gives him time to clearly focus on the objective and to build a stronger desire to retrieve it.

Fetch!

You can train your dog without him even realizing it!

You'll also need: collar and lead, treats, two identical toys, a clicker (optional)

You'll also need: a ball, treats, a clicker (optional)

Drop!

When it's time to let go...

'Drop' is one of the most important commands to teach your dog, not only for your convenience but also for his safety. One day he may grab something that he shouldn't, and you will be glad you took the time to teach him to let go on command. It's also useful on an everyday basis when playtime or bone-chewing time is over and you want to retrieve the toys or bones without unnecessary fuss.

Choose a toy and play with your dog. When he has it in his mouth, hold a tasty treat right in front of his nose and say 'Drop'. If you've selected the right treat, he will open his mouth to take it and the toy will fall out. Timing is of the essence here, and you must say 'Drop' at exactly the same time as his mouth starts to open. Click, praise him, giving him lots of fuss and reward him with the treat.

Give your dog lots of opportunities over the course of several days to trade a toy for a treat, while you use the same command. With repetition, he will learn to associate mouth opening with the command 'Drop'.

When you feel confident, try the command without holding the treat in front of his nose. If you've trained enough, he should drop the toy. Now offer the treat after he has let go of the toy. Eventually, he will drop the object without the treat.

Or try this: Give your dog a favourite toy to drop. If he lets go of something he really wants, it will show you how well trained he has become.

Did you know that you can train your dog to find specific items such as his toys?

Take one item, such as a tennis ball. Let your dog touch the ball and say, 'Touch ball!', so you get his attention on the ball while simultaneously teaching him what it is called. Emphasise the word 'ball'. After five repetitions, take the ball and hide it under a towel or cushion. Now tell him to 'Find the ball'. When he finds it, praise him, pop a treat in his mouth, and let him play with the ball. Repeat this exercise a few times, but remember to hide the ball in different places. Help your dog search if you need to, but let him find it on his own as much as possible.

Or try this: Once your dog can find the ball on command, play the game with other items that he can learn by name. This is fun and mentally challenging for him. He has to think and that's always good; it's also a very useful skill. For example, when you've lost your car keys, you can use your dog's natural and learned abilities by simply saying, 'Find my keys'. Good items to use in this game with are his food bowl, toys, hats and gloves, and – always a favourite – his collar and lead.

Recognition Games

Teach your dog to recognize named objects

You'll also need: objects (ball, lead, bowl), a towel or cushion, treats

You'll also need: family and friends, treats

The Name Game

He can find a ball but can he find Mum?

This is a natural progression from asking your dog to find objects by name. Now you are going to teach him how to recognize (and find) people.

Ask a family member or friend to show your dog a treat. As you hold him, the person should walk away to another part of the garden or, if you're playing indoors, into another room. Let your dog watch the person (and the treat) walk away. When the person has found a place to hide, tell your dog to 'Find Peter!' and let go of his collar. If he finds Peter, praise him. Peter should give him the treat as soon as he reaches him. As you follow him, continue praising him. Repeat five times, or until your dog becomes bored of the game.

After a break, repeat the steps but ask Peter to go somewhere different each time. Gradually, with practice, make the searches harder. When found, the person should always offer a treat immediately, and you must follow the dog, praising him.

Or try this: When your dog can find Peter, begin all over again with another family member – 'Find Diane!'. He will eventually remember as many people as you ask him to.

You'll also need: collar and lead, agility jumps (bought or home-made from boxes, logs, buckets and garden poles), cones, treats, a clicker (optional), a whistle (optional)

Run, Jump, Weave

Make your own agility course

As well as being fun, this training game is a valuable tool for teaching your dog some basic obedience. Start by planning your course. Try to include a couple of jumps – you can create these by placing garden canes on up-turned buckets. Find a wide piece of wood to use as a ramp and arrange some cones or garden canes standing in buckets of soil for weaving poles.

With your dog on the lead, blow your whistle or give the command 'Go'. Run with him around the course, encouraging him along the way (alternatively, use the clicker each time he clears a jump or gets a weave right). Your aim is to get your dog over the jumps, running across the ramp, and weaving in and out of the poles. This will take some time and practice, so start off with a low ramp and position the poles fairly wide apart for the weave. Persevere with this 'on the lead' training until he shows signs of knowing what to do. The next step is to ask him to sit at the start of the course and then remove the lead. Blow the whistle or give a release command and see what happens. Try to always run alongside him, as this really is a team effort. If you wish, you can ask a family member or friend to stand at the other end of the course to shout encouragement. If, at any point, your dog looks bored, stop immediately and try again another time. As he improves and gets faster, try timing him to see if he can beat his own record.

Or try this: As part of the course, make a dog walk. Use three pieces of wide wood and two up-turned buckets. Build a ramp up to the first bucket, a flat ramp going across to the second bucket, and a ramp down from the second bucket. Make sure the ramp is safe and no more than twice the height of your dog. These are great fun and also make good up-and-over (or under) obstacles.

15

You'll also need: treats, children (optional)

Simon Says...

Your dog can join in the fun

This fun activity teaches your dog obedience and to focus all his attention on you when you ask him to do so.

This is a great game for children, as the dog will most certainly pick up on what they are doing. Ask your participants to stand in a row and then stand in front of them. Start by saying, 'Simon says sit'. This is hopefully a command that you have already taught your dog, so emphasize the word 'sit' in the same way as if you were using it as a command. If your dog does it straight away, throw him a treat. Now you can try 'Simon says hands up'. As everyone follows you, go over to the dog and take his paw, lifting it gently up. Praise him with a treat. Let the children get involved as much as possible. Once you have got the basics under your belt, try the following: lie down, crawl, beg, and shake hands.

It's important to keep the rules simple and be realistic. It's not going to work if you say, 'Simon says put your hands on your head'. Start with some of the things your dog has already been taught.

Or try this: If your dog seems to be struggling, why not let him play the role of leader with you? Let him sit by your side and watch the others. You can still encourage him and then let him join in again at a later stage.

16

You'll also need: a few favourite toys, various food treats, a stopwatch (optional)

Temptation Alley

Can your dog resist the treats along the way?

The name of this game says it all here: can you get your dog to travel along a pathway that is littered with some of his favourite things and ignore them all? This is a great activity and fantastic training.

All you need is an area that will enable your dog to begin at one end and finish up at the other. Lay out the course with some treats and toys when your dog is not around, scattering things randomly on either side of his 'alley'.

Ask a friend to hold your dog at one end while you stand at the other end (the finishing line). When you are ready, use the recall (call his name), so that he has to run from one end of the alley to the other. The aim of the game is to get him to the finishing line without stopping to eat treats or pick up toys along the way.

To make the game even more challenging, try putting a few obstacles in his way – perhaps a couple of small jumps or a tunnel. This will make your dog stop and think, but will he still pass up on the treats to win the game?

Or try this: This is a great game when played with friends and their dogs. The winner is the dog with the least distractions at the end. To make it more challenging, gradually move the treats and toys closer together. You can also time it to make it even more fun. Treats at the end, of course!

This game is a good way to teach your dog self-control, and will also give you the peace of mind that he can sit and stay on command. The aim is to see if your dog can remain still, even when you drop coins on the floor. His natural instinct will be to move forward to see what you have dropped – is it a tasty treat? A dog's instinct when you drop something is to investigate it; they are the nosiest creatures on earth.

Ask your dog to sit and move a little way away from him, maybe three or four steps at first. Next, hold a coin in the air and drop it. Watch his face: his entire attention will be on you and whatever you have dropped, especially as coins make such a racket when they hit a hard floor. At this point, repeat the word 'Stay'. You need him to keep still and only move when you say so. It might not work at first, but don't worry. As with most games, it will take time and patience on your part. Always reward and praise your dog if he manages to sit and stay for 15 seconds or more. Gradually extend the period of time he has to stay.

Or try this: Once you feel that your instructions are more important than whatever has been dropped on the floor, move farther away and try dropping other things, maybe objects that are closer to your dog's heart such as toys. If you are feeling really brave, try a favourite treat – a sure test of his willpower.

Drop the Penny

Testing the sit and stay skills

18

You'll also need: coins, treats

You'll also need: 3–4 plastic cups, treats

Be a Magician

Try the cup game for great mental work

The aim of this game is to stimulate your dog mentally. He needs to pay close attention to what you are doing and obey your commands.

Begin by placing the plastic cups upside-down on the ground and put a treat under one of the cups, making sure that your dog sees where it is going. Shuffle the cups around a few times.

Now ask your dog to find the treat. Wait until he gives you a sign that he knows which cup is covering the treat, either by pawing it, sitting next to it, lying by it, or even barking at it. Don't let him get at the treat; just allow him to indicate which cup is hiding it.

As soon as you are happy that he is indicating the correct cup, lift it up and let him have the treat. Once your dog understands what is required of him, you can make it harder by adding more cups before you ask him to find the treat, or you might pretend to place it under all of the cups. Another way is to set up the cups while your dog is in another room, then call him and let him make his choice.

Or try this: If your dog enjoys the cup game, why not make it even harder for him? Use saucepans instead of cups, or place the treats in sealed containers (not clear ones). This will make the game more challenging and the end result will be more worthwhile.

Boredom Busters

A bored dog, much like a bored person, can soon become fed up with life in general. Many of us associate a happy dog with one that has lots of physical exercise, but to keep your best friend really happy, you need to stimulate him mentally as well. Games that involve both physical and mental agility will give him a full workout for both mind and body. And guess what? You do not need to take hours out of your day to provide adequate amounts of mental stimulation. If you start playing these games regularly, you will probably notice that your dog appears more settled, less restless, less hyperactive and less attention-seeking – and he won't need massive amounts of physical exercise just to make him tolerable to be around. Balance is the key. Some of the games in this section even allow you to kill two birds with one stone (mental stimulation and physical exercise together).

You'll also need: a flying disc, treats

Fun with a Flying Disc

Flying high

Most dogs love to chase things. In fact, for many the act of chasing something that is moving fast is instinctive. Start by tossing the flying disc a few metres and encouraging your dog to fetch and bring it back to you. Encouragement is the key word here. If he doesn't instinctively chase the disc show him what to do! Go to fetch it and he will follow.

To encourage him to bring it back, bend down, pat your knees and shout 'Fetch'. Don't worry if he doesn't understand immediately – if you persevere and offer a treat the first time he brings it, he will soon learn.

As your dog learns to fetch the disc, you can start throwing it a little farther and higher. Many dogs love to catch a disc in mid-air. Why not turn it into a competition if you have two dogs or more, and see who can get back first with their prize?

Or try this: It doesn't have to be a flying disc that you throw for your dog. You can use a tennis ball, a plastic container lid or even a plastic plate. Instead of throwing the ball, try rolling it using the same principles.

20

For both dogs and humans, a walk is refreshing, mentally stimulating and a great way to exercise the heart, lungs and legs. This game uses different speeds to make your walk more interesting. Start off by varying the pace at which you walk: for example walk at your normal speed for a few minutes, then speed up with a bit of power-walking, before slowing down again. Your dog will love this new 'game' and will probably end up looking at your feet and face for his next cue to go faster!

Try some speed-test games; ask a family member or friend to hold your dog while you walk (or run) away from him. Then, bend down and call your dog's name as your friend lets go of him: time how long it takes for him to run to you. Praise him and give him a treat when he reaches you.

If you enjoy jogging, why not let your dog run beside you? He will enjoy the training as much as you do.

Or try this: It might sound strange, but a really good game is to run backwards and let your dog run towards you. He will enjoy being face-to-face with you. Try running with his favourite toy in your hand, as this will hold his attention. Just be careful not to trip up!

Fast and Furious!

Racing against your buddy

21

You'll also need: a collar and lead, stopwatch (optional)

You'll also need: a toy, treats

Zig and Zag

The darting game

Following on from 'Fast and Furious', try the 'zig and zag' game. It's good exercise for both you and your dog, and a great way to bond.

Start by encouraging your dog to engage with you on a one-to-one basis. Do this by shouting his name, clapping your hands or waving a toy.

You then need to run – erratically! Dart from left to right, reverse your direction and maybe jump over a small bush or run around a tree or pole (I told you it would be good for you!).

Your dog will love the element of surprise, and will be wondering what you are going to do next; this will keep his attention focused on you for as long as you want.

A guarantee that he will do what you want is to have a treat concealed in your hand. Always praise him and give him the treat as a reward for a job well done.

Or try this: Ask a friend with a dog to walk with you, then both do the activity together. Set off in different directions and watch your dogs have fun deciding who to run with and which way to go.

You'll also need: a toy, a handkerchief, treats

Keep on Track

It's a nose thing

A dog's sense of smell is incredible, and this game puts it to good use. In this activity – known as tracking – you can let your dog use his nose to have fun. First, choose a toy or a handkerchief with your scent on it.

This game works best if your dog is off the lead, so only try it if you have good control over him. If you feel uncertain, first try some of the training games from the training chapter, or use a lead with a long line.

Choose an area where there are places, such as bushes, walls and benches, to hide items. Ask a family member or friend to hold your dog and distract him while you hide the objects.

Go back to your dog and walk towards the first 'hidden' object. Encourage him to use his nose to find it. Some dogs may 'track' – or follow – your footsteps, as they find the smell and use it to trace the treasure. Others may pick up the drifting scent of the object and literally follow their nose.

This is great mental stimulation for your dog, and an effective way for you to watch the very essence of what makes a dog, well, a dog!

Or try this: If there are a few adults and children spare, get them to hide with the treats. That way it's fun for all the family. You don't have to use treats every time – simply use lots of affection and verbal praise to reward your dog when he finds you.

This is a very engaging game, and one that both children and your dog will really enjoy – indoors or outside in the garden.

Use the beam of your torch as a fun object for your dog to pounce on. Let him get used to you darting the light around on the ground, then watch as he realizes that the aim of the game is to jump on the light. Shout encouragement at all times – shout 'Get it' and your dog will associate the phrase with this particular game. Don't forget that your enthusiasm is the best way to encourage him to play. Use treats to reward him when he successfully jumps on a beam.

Dogs are easily drawn into this game and, before you know it, your dog will be lungeing at the light, which you can then move to another point – suddenly. You can even shine your torch up a wall or tree, but watch out for the barking if your dog becomes excited, as you don't want to annoy your neighbours.

Or try this: Shine the torch on the floor and let your dog follow patterns – circles, figures of eight and round your body. Alternatively hide the torch under things and let your dog find it – guaranteed fun for both of you.

Shine a Light

Beam me up, Scottie

You'll also need: a torch, treats

You'll also need: a remote-controlled toy, treats

Remote Control

Toy box antics

Chasing a moving object is the aim of this game. You can use a remote-controlled car or robot – or any other toy that can be moved independently.

Get your dog interested in the toy by using the remote control to make it move, and wait until you have his full attention. You could even place a dog treat on the toy to get him really excited.

Encourage your dog to chase the toy, and then reward him with praise and treats. I can guarantee that this will soon become a favourite game. This activity can be adapted if you have more than one dog; watch how competitive they become when there is a 'prize' involved, but stop the game immediately if there is any sign of aggression.

Or try this: Why not let your children or other family members control the toys? The winner is the one whose dog gets the most treats in a certain amount of time, perhaps five minutes.

This is a variation on the classic game of hide-and-seek that we humans enjoy so much. You may be surprised to find that your dog loves playing it as much as you do.

There are two ways of playing dog hide-and-seek: either you can get a friend or family member to hold your dog or you can ask them to shut him in a room briefly. All you have to do then is to hide. It's that simple. If you have more than one dog, they can hunt for you together.

If indoors (and if your dog is allowed upstairs), try hiding under the bed, in a wardrobe or behind a slightly open door. Good places downstairs include behind the sofa, in the downstairs lavatory or under a table. Make sure you have a treat ready for when your dog finds you.

Most dogs are great at this game, because of their great sense of smell and natural instinct to explore. If your dog is slow getting started, call his name quietly – he'll soon get the hang of it.

Or try this: Remember that your dog will get to know your usual hiding places, so it is important to vary them as much as you can. If outdoors, you can use trees, walls and cars to hide behind, but just make sure it's safe to do so.

Hide-and-Seek

Coming...ready or not!

You'll also need: treats

You'll also need: cooked sausage pieces (or other tasty treats), whistle (optional)

Seek the Sausage!

A fun variation on hide-and-seek

This is a really simple twist on the previous game. Instead of hiding yourself, you conceal pieces of cooked sausage (or similar strong-smelling treats) around the house.

Begin by shutting your dog in a room so that he can't see where you are hiding the treats – think of good places and areas to conceal them to stretch him mentally. Under rugs, behind chairs and on low window-ledges are good places to start. If you want to hide treats under pillows or in laundry baskets, wrap them in some tissue paper or a plastic freezer-bag.

Always let your dog know when the game has started – you can use a whistle and the command 'Find'. If he needs a little help initially, give it to him. As he gets more accustomed to playing this game, you can gradually become more inventive with your hiding places.

Be careful if you are playing this with more than one dog. One treat and two dogs can often end in sulks!

Or try this: Dogs have a great 'digging' instinct and will love to find anything that has been buried, so hide a treat beneath an old cushion or a pile of newspapers.

You'll also need: a large bowl or bucket, balls, old newspapers, cooked sausages (or other tasty treats)

Treat Bobbing

A great party or Halloween trick

Apple-bobbing is often associated with Halloween but this canine version doesn't have to be played at Halloween. It's fun if there is more than one dog, so if you can't get any dog-owning friends round, toss some apples in as well and have an adult and dog bobbing contest.

Fill the bucket or bowl with lots of clean water, so it is deep enough for your treats to float easily on top and to create a challenge for the person (or dog) try ing to get them. Place the bucket on some old newspapers and fill with dog treats. If you don't fancy sharing a bucket with the dogs, have a separate one for humans.

Bring the dogs to the container and let them have a sniff: they will realize that there are treats inside

One dog at a time (or one person at a time) bends down to the water and tries to catch a treat using only their mouths. Give a time limit of 45 seconds to a minute for each turn. Dogs who fish out the treats get to eat them.

Just be careful that there is no jealousy over treats if several dogs are playing, and never let more than one dog have a go at the same time, unless you are 100 per cent sure they won't fight over the prizes.

Or try this: If you don't want a wet floor, try treat bobbing in sand or by wrapped items in screwed-up paper. Hide some treats in the sand (a bit like a tombola) and let the children and dog feel their way round to find a human (or canine) treat.

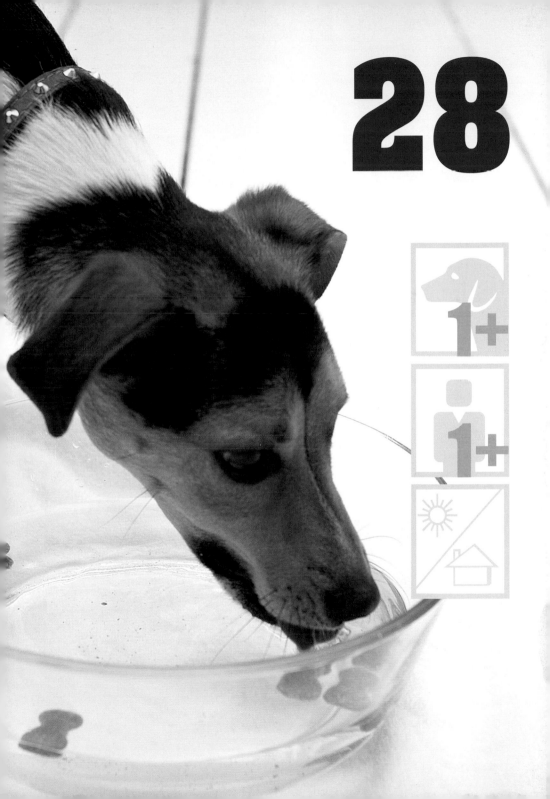

28

You'll also need: collar and lead, treats

Up and Over

Weave, leap, twist and turn

A park, field, or some open countryside are all ideal places to teach your dog the basics of agility. He will undoubtedly love the challenge, and you will be surprised at how easy it is to find 'obstacles' for him during your walks – trees, gates, low walls and perhaps some large rocks. These can all become your dog's natural agility course.

Weaving: Keep your dog on the lead at first and use plenty of encouragement and treats to steer him towards some trees. Lead him in and out of the trees in a weave, praising him all the time. He will soon understand what is required and then you can speed up. When you feel more confident (this may take days, rather than hours), let him off the lead and ask him to follow you. He should naturally progress to the point where he can do this on his own, with a tasty treat as a reward.

Jumping: If your dog is over 12 months old you can teach him to jump. Again, find a natural 'fence' somewhere – this could be a large branch, a small fallen tree, or even a narrow stream. Start off with your dog on the lead and jump with him to begin with, if you are able to. Gradually speed up so he jumps more quickly. When he can do this, let him off the lead and encourage him to do it on his own – and don't forget to reward success with treats.

Or try this: If you don't have easy access to open areas, don't worry. This game can be played on an urban walk on a smaller scale. Look for objects that your dog can jump over, such as low walls, or things he can weave around, like street lamps, or you can even use the lines in the pavement. It has to be done on the lead, of course, but it will still be a great game for your dog.

up. Get your dog to walk around you in a circle by holding out a treat for him to follow. Do this in a clockwise direction and then repeat anti-clockwise.

Hold a large hoop low to the ground and encourage your dog to trot backwards and forwards and jump through it, giving him a treat each time he succeeds. If he manages this, and is over 12 months old, hold a treat up in the air and get him to jump up on his back legs. Do this no more than five times because it may be hard on his joints.

Lastly, hold out a long stick or brush handle, about 7.5 cm (3 in) off the ground (you may need a friend to help you), and get your dog to jump backwards and forwards, using a treat to encourage him. This is the aerobic part of the workout and it should last for about three minutes. Repeat the rubbing-down session with the cloth as a cool-down at the end of the workout.

Make sure your dog is content and calm. Start rubbing him with a soft cloth. Work your way down one side in firm, straight movements, and repeat on the other side, then work your way down his legs. Praise him all the time and use treats to reward and encourage him when necessary. Next, do a warm-

Or try this: Hold a treat close to the dog's nose and lure his head round to encourage gentle stretching from side to side and up and down.

Workouts and Woofs

How to have a healthy hound

You'll also need: a soft cloth, a hoop, a long stick or brush handle, treats

You'll also need: a ball, treats

Work Out Together

How to get healthy with your dog

Why not get fit while you're walking your dog? Go to a safe, open space where you can let your dog off the lead, if possible. Stop and do some simple stretches to get your limbs working and your heart pumping. Do some lunges, twists and upper-body twists. As you are doing your workout, allow your dog to run around you. Let him be inquisitive and if he feels like jumping up as you stretch your arms up, encourage him to do so.

Run around in circles for a while and let him chase you and maybe do a quick sprint now and again with him. There's no need for anything too taxing here, but it's a guaranteed way for both of you to make the most of your daily walk. Remember to use treats, if necessary, as a way of rewarding your dog.

It is important to keep this activity safe for both of you, so don't allow your dog to jump up at inappropriate moments or to get under your feet and trip you up. Your common sense will dictate when he can and can't participate, so use the ball to distract him if he is likely to get in the way.

Or try this: If you can't get outdoors, do some simple exercises at home. Why not have a crazy 15-minute dance around the room to some of your favourite music and let your dog join in? He can have fun running and bounding around with you for a great cardio-workout.

Play tunnels are an easy way for your dog to have fun, especially if he has other 'friends' who can get involved. Tunnels can become an enjoyable and important part of racing and hide-and-seek games, and are often used in agility.

Firstly, you need to find some large boxes. Open the bottoms and tops of each box and lay them next to each other. Tape them together securely on all sides to make a tunnel large enough for your dog to get through comfortably. You can start with a tunnel made from two or three boxes, and then gradually make it longer as your dog grasps what is required of him and starts having fun.

Lead your dog to the tunnel, then race to the other end and call him through. He may need lots of encouragement initially. Try running to the mouth of the tunnel, encouraging him to go through as you run along the outside. If necessary, ask a friend to hold the dog while you call him through. Give him a treat when he gets to you, and gradually introduce the word 'tunnel'. Give him a treat when he runs through the tunnel. This is a very rewarding game for both of you.

Or try this: If the cardboard boxes are sturdy enough, try placing one end of your tunnel on some bricks or books to raise it. Or use the play tunnels that you can buy from toy stores...then you can involve your kids, too!

Tackle a Tunnel

Dogs love this...and it's easy to make

32

You'll also need: cardboard boxes, sticky tape, treats

You'll also need: treats, a clicker (optional)

High-Five!

Teach your dog to touch your hand

Your dog's affection for you will be a useful ally when you are teaching this trick, because many dogs offer their paw quite spontaneously to express affection.

With your dog in a sit, kneel down in front of him with a treat hidden in your hand. Hold the treat hand out so he can smell it and move your hand slightly so that he has to shift his weight from the paw you want him to lift. If he lifts his paw to get the treat, click (if using) and reward. If he is reluctant, gently tickle the paw so that he lifts it, then click and treat. Keep practising and gradually add on the words 'high five' or 'paw'.

Shaking someone's hand and giving someone a high-five are virtually indistinguishable to your dog, so you can use the same command for the same reaction. Always respond to him when he tries this by offering your raised palm; this will be his reassurance that he has hit his target, especially if he gets a treat at the same time. Persevere with this – it's a great and very simple trick. Ask other members of the family to practise with the dog, too. The more times he does it, the sooner he will become proficient.

Or try this: When your dog can perform a high-five on command with you kneeling down, you can progress to doing it when you are standing up.

Children are often shouted at to tidy their toys, but did you realize that what may be a chore for a child is a great game for your dog? In fact, if you work at this hard enough, you may never have to pick up your dog's toys again.

To play this game, you will need one of your dog's favourite toys and the box in which you keep them. Make sure that the toy box is in sight and within easy reach. Place the toy on the floor and ask your dog to 'Fetch' the toy.

As soon as he picks it up, kneel by his toy box and call him. Ask him to 'Give' the toy, and make sure he sees you drop it into the box. Praise him and reward him with a treat. Repeat this exercise until he can take the toy to the box and drop it in himself. Be patient – it will take practice before he gets it right every time.

Or try this: When your dog can tidy away a specific toy, you can progress to two toys before scattering three or four toys in different parts of the room. Eventually, you will be able to shout your commands and watch as he tidies his own toys away.

Time to Tidy

Putting things away is fun – honestly!

You'll also need: toys, a toy box, treats

You'll also need: collar and lead, balls, treats

Puppy Love

Arrange a play date for your dog!

This is a real boredom-buster for you and your canine pal and a fun and very effective way of socializing puppies and young dogs.

Choose a fine day for this, whatever the season. Arrange to meet up with a friend and her dog in a place where it will be safe to let them off their leads. There's no big deal to this activity; it's just a great way to enable your dog to play with another dog, and you can catch up with friends or family at the same time. Make sure that both your dogs are on their leads for the first part of the walk, especially if they have never met before. They will soon be friends for life.

Praise your dogs lavishly and, when you feel confident, let them off the lead. Encourage them to run together, throw balls for them, and treat them both the same – if one gets a treat for good behaviour, then reward the other dog, too.

If there is any animosity between the two dogs, which is unlikely, put them back on their leads and make them walk together for a few more minutes. Often, having one dog on a lead and the other running free can trigger threatening behaviour; this

is natural and can be easily addressed by ensuring you treat all the dogs equally.

Or try this: If you don't have a friend with a dog, you could take your dog to training classes or canine activities. Of course, you may make new friends if you walk your dog regularly in a public park or any other open space.

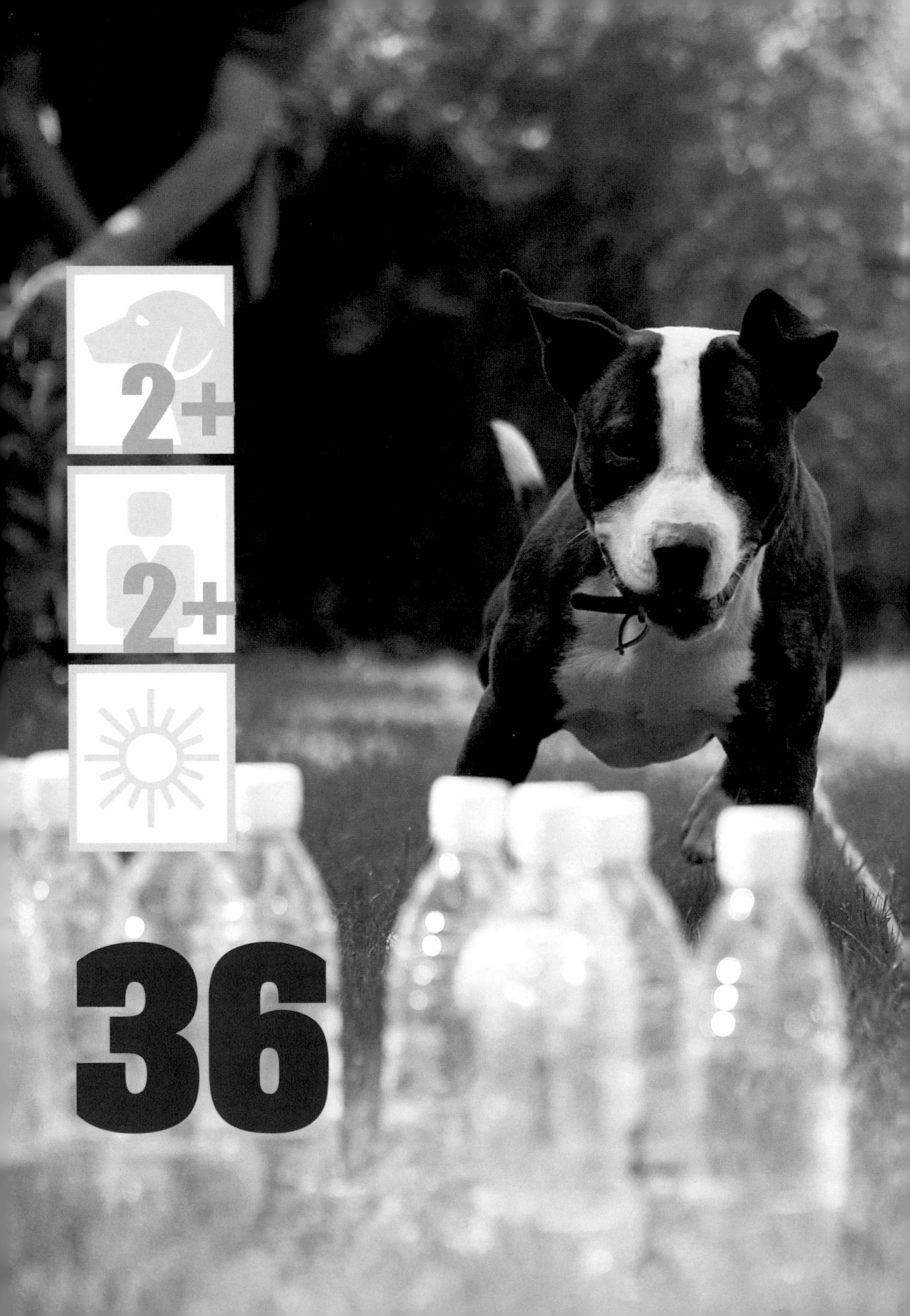
2+
2+
36

You'll also need: several wooden planks or garden poles, empty plastic bottles, a tennis ball, a score sheet, treats

Kingpin!

Bowling alley canine madness

In this game your dog is the 'bowling ball' and the aim is to see how many plastic bottles he can knock down in one go!

Line up your planks of wood or garden poles in parallel lines to create an alley. Try to make it as long as possible, depending on where you are playing, of course. At the end of your alley, line up 10 plastic bottles in a triangle: four at the back, three in front of them, then another two in the next row, and one at the front.

This game is simple: each team member throws a ball a little higher than the tops of the bottles. The dog then chases the ball and, hopefully, in doing so knocks the bottles down. He may well try to jump over the bottles at first, but any time he does knock some – or all – of the bottles over, praise him loudly and offer him a treat. He'll soon get the hang of it.

Set the bottles back up again and let the next team have a go. Ask someone to stand by with a score sheet to note down how many bottles were knocked down. The team that have knocked over the most number of bottles at the end of a set number of rounds are the winners: treats for all!

Or try this: Encourage each dog to not only knock down the bottles but also bring them back to you. The owner with the most retrieved bottles at the end of the game is the winner. Each bottle brought back earns your dog a treat.

Family Fun

The activities in this chapter include the whole family: games your dog can enjoy with the children, with you and with your wider family and friends. Dogs and kids usually have a special bond, but do monitor them as they play. Any games and activities will be fun provided that your children are aware of the following: they must always be gentle with the dog, never pull on the dog's tail and never mess around with the dog when he is eating, sleeping or going to the toilet. Also teach them to praise or reward the dog every time he does as he is told. This will strengthen the bond between the dog and the child and teach the dog to respect the child's authority. The reward doesn't always have to be something edible – it may simply be a stroke, a pat on the head or a kind word. When activities are planned with friends and their dogs, make sure that the dogs have been properly introduced beforehand.

You may struggle to get the required nine players, but don't worry because this is doggy baseball and different rules apply. Set up a rough baseball pitch with three bases in a triangular shape (this is a simple game of baseball, not major league). The bigger the area you can set up without losing sight of the dogs or players, the better. The purpose of each game is to score points, called 'runs'. The team with the most runs at the end of the game wins.

You need a batter and a pitcher: the batter to hit the ball and the pitcher to throw it. Anyone else on the team is a fielder. The aim of the game is for the batter to hit the ball as far as he can and try to get round all of the bases without being out.

Now, here's where the dog comes in! When the ball is hit, encourage the dog (or dogs) to go after the ball and bring it back, so you can hit a base and stop the runner. Most dogs will instinctively run for the ball; all you have to do is get them to give it to you! Don't forget to encourage your dog, and if you have trained your dog you can use the command 'Fetch'. Keep some treats on your person so that you can reward the dog once you've got the batter out!

Or try this: If you don't have access to all of the props that are necessary for this game, simply use a ball and a bat – you could even use a lump of wood. Then all you need is someone to toss the ball and another person to hit it; it's the dog's job to chase it and bring it back.

Go, Joe DiMaggio!

Baseball heaven for dogs

You'll also need: a ball, three bases (buckets, cones or bricks), a bat, treats

You'll also need: water, a whistle (optional)

Tag Time

Who will win this fast-paced game?

This favourite children's game is easy to adapt, so that your dog can join in as well. To start, decide who is going to be 'it'. It's perhaps best at this point to choose one of the human players, until the dog gets the hang of the game. The person who is 'it' has to give all the other players a 10–15 second head start to run as far away as they can, then the 'it' person has to give chase and tag the first player they catch.

Set the boundaries for the game before you start. You require quite a large area for the game to be real fun – a park or open field is ideal. Let the players know where the 'edges' of the game are and don't let anyone run past that point. Part of the fun is darting around and avoiding the dreaded 'tag': the point at which the person chasing touches another person or dog, making them 'it' in turn. Time this game in one-minute long sessions, the person (or dog!) who is 'it' when the whistle blows is the loser of that game and must sit out until a new game starts. The aim is to have one winner at the end of all the games.

This is a fast game, so make sure you have water for the dog and drinks for the children. The game can be stopped at any time for a break and resumed when you are ready.

Or try this: Make the game even more riotous and fun by playing it with more than one dog. Even though it may get a little confusing at times, everyone will enjoy themselves.

You'll also need: treats

Ring of Rovers!

Round and round the circle he goes...

This is another variation on a classic children's game that can be enjoyed by both adults and dogs as well. In fact, the more people who take part, the better it is. Start by forming a circle: if there are only four or so people, stand well apart – the more players there are, the closer together they need to stand.

Each player should have a treat in their hand and a couple of spare ones in their pockets. If possible, get your dog to sit still in the middle of the ring, but don't worry if he's excited and won't do this.

Point at the person whom you want to go first and ask them to shout the dog's name. When he gets to them, they must give him a treat. Now get your dog back into the middle of the ring once more. Note that if the dog does not move towards the caller within five seconds, the caller is out and must leave the circle.

Slowly all move together in your circle and tell the dog to 'Sit'. Now point to a different person and ask them to call the dog. Again, when he gets to them they should give him the treat they are holding. The game is won by the last person standing with the dog.

Or try this: If there are only three or four of you, try standing in a triangle or a square and playing the same game.

39

Tennis is enjoyed the world over, so why not play it at home with your dog? You never know, he may be the next big tennis star!

This game is ideally played against a wall, as it makes it easier for you and your family or friends (as well as the dog) to keep close to each other during play. The idea is simple: it's the humans' job to hit the tennis balls against the wall, and the dog's job to retrieve the ball when one of you misses. If you are using a net, play in exactly the same way: one or more humans on either side and the dog plays at being ball boy. Make sure that he knows it's his job to bring the ball back to you and not to run away with it. Reward him with treats and verbal praise when he gives you the ball.

This is a great game and it gets you fit at the same time. Some dogs bark a lot during tennis, but don't worry about this – they are just enjoying themselves.

Or try this: If you don't have tennis rackets handy, throw a ball against a wall and let it bounce back to the dog to catch. You could count how many bounces it takes – and try to improve on this each time you play the game.

Anyone for Tennis?

Train your dog to be a ball boy

40

You'll also need: a tennis ball, tennis racket (at least one), a wall (optional), net (optional), treats

You'll also need: a list of items, a ball, treats

I Spy...

...with my little eye!

This game is a great way to liven up a walk with children and your dog. It doesn't matter whether you're going for a stroll through the park or just around the block, because you can make the rules up as you go along.

Before you set off on the walk, make a list of ten things you want the children to find, such as a feather, flower, stone or pebble, candy-wrapper or blade of grass. Obviously, tailor the list to things that you know will be available, but don't make it too easy. Give each child a copy of the list and provide them with a small empty bucket or bag. Pop a ball and some treats for your dog in your pocket.

Tell the children they have to look for as many of the items as possible and collect them during the walk. Make sure they respect people's property. Meanwhile, at some point on the walk, hide the dog's treats or ball a little further ahead (sneak off while the kids are looking for things with the dog). This is his playtime, so encourage him to 'sniff out' his prize as you get near to it.

When you arrive home from your walk, ask the children to count how many things they have and

tick them off their list; the winner is the person with the most ticks.

Or try this: A little harder but just as much fun, ask the children to find things beginning with certain letters of the alphabet or ask them to find as many things as they can of the same colour.

Have fun with this popular game, in which your dog becomes a bingo-caller for the day (with a little help from his friends, of course).

Here's what to do: number 50 cardboard squares from 1 to 50 and fold each around a small dog treat. Put all the folded cards into a large bowl and give them a good toss around so they are mixed up evenly. On the blank pieces of paper (one per player), write down ten random numbers between 1 and 50. Make sure each piece of paper has different numbers, although it's OK if a couple have a pair of identical numbers.

Next, each player takes a sheet of paper and a pen. Now all that's needed is your bingo-caller. Offer the bowl to your dog and let him choose one card from the bowl (you may need to help at first). When he has picked one out, unwrap it and give him the treat. You now have your first number and he has his reward for doing his job properly. Call out the number on the card to the players. If anyone has that number written down on their sheet of paper, they must cross it off. Repeat this with your dog (not forgetting to treat him each time) until someone has

crossed off all ten numbers on their sheet. They must then shout 'Bingo' or 'House'. The winner receives a prize. This is a great game for a rainy day, and you can play as many rounds as you want.

Or try this: As there are a lot of treats involved in this game, choose healthy ones and cut them into very small pieces – you don't want an overweight bingo-caller.

Bingo!

Go for a full-house

You'll also need: 50 squares of thin blank card (each about the size of your palm), paper and pens, a large bowl, tiny dog treats, prizes

43

You'll also need: treats for the dog, treats for the children, a whistle (optional)

Hide and Treat

Surprises galore for all the family

This is a good game to play in an area where there are lots of hiding places. The aim is to hide treats for the dog and the children and see who finds them first. Who will win – the dogs or the humans?

An optimum amount of treats for the dog is perhaps five or six, with the same number for each of the children. Try to leave sufficient amounts of space around each dog treat, as your dog's sense of smell will give him a distinct advantage over the humans. Remember that praise is always good when the dog finds his treasure and it's OK for him to eat it straight away if you want him to.

There does not have to be a logical trail; in fact, the crazier the better. You can hide things almost anywhere, but make sure they are in places which their 'sniffers' can reach easily: remember that dogs can't climb trees! When playing this game for the first time, make the hiding places fairly obvious. Once everyone understands the game, put the treats somewhere more challenging.

Once the treats are hidden, you can either call the dog(s) and children or blow a whistle. If the dogs take a little time to work out what is required,

never mind. Help them to find the first treat, then encourage them in the general direction of the next one and so on.

Or try this: Put the treats in your pockets and then hide yourself. Get someone else to start the game when you are safely hidden.

44

You'll also need: old sheets, scissors, a black marker pen, a tape measure, treats (pipe-cleaners, fabric dye and fancy-dress horns are optional)

Ghost Busters

Spooky goings-on with your dog

All kids love to dress up, so why not let them involve the dog too? This is a great activity for a rainy day: it will keep the kids occupied for ages and the dog can join in the fun as well. It's fun to make this costume for Halloween: your neighbours will hopefully be amused by a 'spooked-up' dog trick-or-treating at their door.

To make your dog's ghost costume you will need an old sheet, a pair of scissors and a black marker pen for special effects. Measure your dog from the back of his head (just behind the ears) to roughly halfway down his tail. Next, cut out a circle from the sheet that is about the same size in diameter. Place the sheet on the dog and mark a circle where his head is, then cut a hole his head will fit through. Now have a fitting: put the dog's head through the hole and carefully (you may need to ask someone to hold him) cut around the bottom and sides of the sheet to give the costume a ragged appearance. If you are feeling adventurous, use the black marker pen to draw a skeleton effect on the sides with ribs, a backbone and a skull, for example.

Or try this: Create a spider: fit the sheet in the same way, then dye it black or colour it black all over. Next, get eight large pipe-cleaners (or bendy straws) and colour them black, too. Attach four of these to each side of the sheet to complete the costume. There are all sorts of fancy-dress ideas for dogs, and you really can let your imagination run riot (as long as the dog is not made to be an object of fun, is involved and enjoying himself, and is able to eat, drink and go to the toilet while wearing the costume). Try local pet shops or look on the Internet for outfits. Some baby clothes will fit smaller dogs, and many dogs are happy to wear a comfortable pair of sunglasses or a hat.

Garden Games

Your dog probably spends a lot of time in your garden or backyard and the activities in this chapter will help you to make the most of his time there. Playing in the garden shouldn't be a substitute for a walk, but you can have lots of fun there. So that your dog can play safely outside, make sure that fences are secure and gates are shut. You may be able to designate a corner of your garden especially for digging games; soft soil is good for this, or even a pile of sand.

You'll also need: a toy basketball and hoop, treats, a clicker (optional)

Hoop Hound

More fun with hoops!

Set up your basketball hoop and place the basketball on the ground. To get your dog acquainted with the basketball, play around with it for a while. Reward him when he pays attention to the ball, so he knows that this is what he must focus on. Try to encourage him to pick the ball up and carry it. If you click and reward each time he picks the ball up, it will help him learn what you want him to do. Gradually withhold the click until he drops the ball.

When he has learned that picking up the ball is good and that dropping the ball when you click is also good, you are ready to move on to the next phase – introducing the hoop. Now you are going to try to get him to drop the ball near to the hoop. Click or praise him when he gets near it. If he drops it nearby, praise and reward him. If he drops it in, make a real fuss of him.

He will now begin to get the idea and as soon as he does, only click and treat your dog for dropping the ball into the hoop.

Once this skill has been mastered, you can arrange a game with some friends. Try to keep the game as gentle as possible and always use the clicker as support. Don't let the game get too fast and competitive or your dog will become over-excited and confused.

Or try this: If you like the idea of this game but don't have a basketball or a hoop, try teaching him to carry his ball and drop it into a bucket – he'll enjoy it just as much.

Fire as many bubbles as you can and get your dog to jump, run and twist in order to catch as many of them as he can. Start off slowly until he grasps the idea. Shoot a couple of bubbles at a time and shout encouragement to him. Try 'Go get them', which will then become his cue to chase whatever you shoot. This is a good game for more than one dog and it's fun for you watching them chasing after the same bubbles, only to dash off to the next one. Watch their faces as the bubbles pop.

Work your way up to shooting as many as you can in as short a time as possible and watch your dog move. Don't worry if he barks at the bubbles – this is a natural response to the game and is part of the fun for your dog.

At the end of the game make sure he has access to plenty of water (this is a thirsty game) and give him a treat to let him know he has done well.

Bubbles are great fun and dogs love to chase them around and pop them. You can use ordinary bubbles for this, but there are also great meat-flavoured ones formulated especially for dogs, which are available from some pet stores.

Or try this: If you can't get a bubble-gun and meat-flavoured bubbles, you can use a child's pot of bubbles with the small ring inside. It might not taste quite as good but it will have exactly the same 'fun-factor' for the dogs.

Bubblemania

Fun with meaty bubbles

You'll also need: a bubble-gun, meat-flavoured bubbles (optional), water, treats

You'll also need: a bone, treats (a strong-smelling treat if you can't get a bone)

Archaeological Dig!

Become a dinosaur hunter

This game is perfect for letting dogs use their exceptional sense of smell and digging skills. Terriers will particularly enjoy this one.

Show your dog his bone (or treat) and let him have a good sniff. Then make sure he stays somewhere where he cannot see what you are up to while you hide it. Go into the garden with his treat and choose a suitable spot to dig a small hole, about 10 cm (4 in) deep, and place the treat squarely at the bottom. You can wrap it in something if you want – cabbage leaves are ideal, but tissue or some newspaper will do just as well. Fill in the hole with earth and try to replace any turf to make the area look as untouched as possible.

Now call your dog and allow him to start searching the garden. If he still has the scent of the bone, he may well simply use his nose. His natural instinct, once he has located the correct spot, will be to dig. Allow him to do this and he will soon unearth his very own pot of gold. You never know what other items of interest he may dig up at the same time! Give him the bone (or treat) as his reward.

Or try this: You don't have to limit this to just one hole. If you wish, you can bury several items for your dog to unearth (it largely depends on how happy you are to have small areas of your garden excavated).

You'll also need: a dog ball (a soccer ball will burst too easily) or an empty plastic bottle, goalposts, a clicker (optional), treats

Soccer Stars

Soccer on four legs!

Would you believe that your dog could actually be a very useful member of your soccer team? If not, read on! Dogs like playing with balls – anything goes, from moving it around with their paws and wrestling with it to moving it along with their mouth or nose. In this activity, you are going to use rewards to give your dog a rough idea of how to join in with you and your friends.

Set up some goalposts – use the children's or even a couple of bricks or cones set about 2 m (6 ft) apart. First of all, you need to attract your dog's attention and get him to focus on the ball (or plastic bottle). Let your dog have a chew and maybe kick it gently around for him, encouraging him to go for the ball himself. Start to make it challenging for him – who will get to the ball first?

Now it's time to make your dog aware of the goal. Kick the ball gently towards the posts and if it goes in, shout 'Goal'. Try to get your dog to do the same, so his attention is on getting the ball in the goal. This may take some time, but stick with it. Reward all movement towards the goal (use a clicker if you want) and give treats when he gets near to the posts.

Or try this: As your dog begins to understand the game, try kicking the ball towards the post and shouting 'Goal' (use the clicker), and let him do the rest. As soon as he does this, reward and praise him. Now you can start to have a real game, making the distances between him and the goal a little further each time. Include your children or friends and form teams letting the dog have a go on both sides.

48

Hold a hoop in one hand, so that the bottom is just touching the ground. In the other hand, hold a treat. Try to lead your dog through the hoop with the treat, and only give it to him if he goes through the hoop. Repeat this several times from each side.

Now hold the hoop off the ground – only about 1 cm (½ in) at first – and again try to lead your dog through the hoop, only giving him the treat if he goes through it. If he goes around the hoop, make him try again. If your dog just won't do it, put the hoop back on the ground and repeat a few more times. If he jumps through the hoop, then keep repeating this step.

After doing this successfully several times, don't hold out a treat for your dog, but keep it in your pocket and ask him to follow your hand signals only. If he jumps through the hoop, take the treat out of your pocket and reward him. However, if your dog doesn't go through the hoop, use the treats to lead him through the hoop several more times. If your dog is over 12 months old, gradually hold the hoop higher, but always keep it at a height at which your dog can comfortably jump through it.

Or try this: Get your children to join in, either going through the hoop themselves or holding the hoop for the dog.

Happy Hooping

Jumping for joy

49

You'll also need: a large hula-hoop, treats

You'll also need: collar and lead, planks of wood (or garden canes), bricks and small buckets, favourite toy, treats

Jumping Jacks

Bouncy, bouncy bow-wows

A game for dogs over 12 months old. Start with low jumps – a good indication is about the height of about halfway up your dog's legs. Allow your dog room for a run-up; he will need four or five strides on either side of the jump.

One of the best ways to start this is for you to jump over with him by your side. Keep him on a lead and hold a treat in your hand. When you approach the jump, try giving the command 'Over' or 'Up', as once he gets used to this it will be easy to teach him other tricks as well. Once he grasps what is required, throw a favourite toy over the jump and tell him to fetch it. Make a big fuss of him when he jumps over and gradually try a grid of two or three fences. Always reward a jump even if he knocks one down.

Or try this: Get your dog to jump over a human obstacle.

51

A Question of Balance

Let's all teeter...and totter!

A teeter-totter is very similar to a see-saw. When training your dog to walk across the teeter-totter, do be patient. Don't encourage him to race across it at full speed until you are sure he is comfortable with the obstacle and how it moves.

Start with your dog on his lead and introduce him to the teeter-totter slowly. Let him have a good sniff; he has probably never seen anything quite like it before. When you are ready, lead him onto the end that is on the ground, using a treat in front of his nose to get him to walk slowly onto the wood. Go really slowly as you get to the point where the balance will tip. As the teeter-totter tips over encourage your dog to walk slowly down and jump off, using the treat as a bait at all times. As soon as he gets off, reward and praise him.

Gradually allow him more freedom on the lead as he moves over it, but stay close to him just in case. The secret to this activity is to train your dog to only leave the teeter-totter when he has reached the ground, and not to attempt daring leaps from the top. Eventually, he will be able to go it alone.

Or try this: You can make your own teeter-totter with a wide wooden plank, about 4 m (12 ft) long and 30 cm (12 in) wide, plus a barrel and some bricks. Size is important, as the plank needs to pivot on its support, and if the top of the support is too wide it will not allow the correct action. A good support is a small barrel, which you can keep steady with bricks. The teeter-totter also needs to be designed in such a way that when it descends it doesn't happen so quickly that the dog falls off it.

Mental and physical agility, eagerness to please, attention to movement and family fun all combine to make this a real favourite. You may have tried your hand at swingball, but may not have thought of playing it with your dog. It's a great game to get you both outside in the fresh air.

To start, get your dog accustomed to the ball. Swing the ball at him gently a couple of times to attract his attention. When he is in the mood to play, swing the ball and use a command ('Swing' is a good one). If at any point, he tries to jump and catch the ball, click (if using), praise him and give him a treat.

Practise this a couple of times, always praising your dog when he goes for the ball and also when he releases the ball back to you. This game is really good for short bursts of exercise, as it is quite intense and tiring. Make sure you have water available at all times. Eventually, you will be able to have a really good game of swingball together, and you can amaze your friends with your flying dog!

Or try this: You can make your own swingball with a pole, a piece of string and a sturdy ball. The pole needs to be driven into some soil and the ball should be securely attached to the end of the string.

Swing Out!

Flyball...with a twist

You'll also need: a child's swingball, a bat (table tennis bats are perfect), water, treats, a clicker (optional)

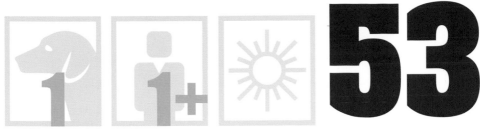

You'll also need: a child's paddling pool, a ball, treats

Splash!

Cool down and have fun

There are not many dogs or children who don't enjoy messing about in water, so combine the two for this activity.

Wait until you have a warm summer's day, and fill a child's paddling pool with water (use warm water if you wish). The pool should be in the centre of the garden and your children suitably dressed to get wet.

You may well find that your dog heads straight for the water; if not, try throwing the ball into the pool and encouraging him to go in after it. Make it a game with the children to see who can get the ball first. However, no one – dogs or children – should get too competitive about trying to get the ball. Keep it light-hearted and fun.

You could also try the 'Ready-Steady-Go' game: just hold the dog and shout 'Ready-Steady-Go', then let go and watch him hit the water making a huge splash.

Or try this: There are now all sorts of plastic slides that you can stand on the ground around paddling pools. Invest in a couple and have sliding competitions, with a treat at the end, of course!

You'll also need: collar and lead, assortment of objects (ball, bottle, pot or toy) of differing shapes and sizes, treats

Touching Base

Canine shapes and sizes

Start by setting out all your objects in a line in the garden, leaving a good space between each – 60 cm (2 ft) is fine. In this game, you are going to ask your dog to copy you. When you approach an object and touch it, he is going to go to the same object and touch it with his nose or paw. Start with him on the lead and walk up to one of your props and bend to touch it. Encourage your dog to touch it straight after or at the same time as you. Use the word 'Touch' as he gets near. When he does this, praise and reward him.

Repeat this a few times, using different items and occasionally going back to the same thing twice, so there is no particular pattern to the game. Remember that this is about him watching what you are doing, not learning a particular routine off by heart. When you feel confident that he has grasped the idea of the game, repeat the activity with him off the lead. Keep him by your side, but this time try to make him do it without actually leading him. As before, use the 'Touch' command and reward and praise each time he gets it right. Ignore him when he gets it wrong and carry on to the next thing.

After a few practice runs (which may take place over several days), go to the next stage. Ask your dog to sit and watch you go up to an object, touch it and walk back to him. Now give the 'Touch' command and see what happens. Hopefully, he will go to the same object and touch it, too. Some dogs will pick the idea up more quickly than others, so be patient and remember that perseverance pays off eventually.

Or try this: Get an old blackboard or large square of wood. Draw different shapes on it with a marker pen or chalk and do the same exercise, but touching the shapes. See if your dog can follow your lead as described above.

Ideas for Breeds

It's a well-known fact that different dog breeds are good at – and enjoy – different sports. Most dogs love to play a wide range of games, but if you have a Terrier you may have noticed his love of digging, whereas if your pet is a Gundog breed, he will probably have an affinity with water. In this chapter, we are going to look at games that are specifically designed with your breed in mind. Hounds, for example, love scent- and sight-related games, while Toy breeds excel at agility-based activities. Working dogs enjoy, well, working! If you own one of the large Working breeds, carting is a great pastime for both of you. Utility breeds, such as the Dalmatian, also enjoy carriage and carting activities, as well as mental games. These games are only suggestions, however, and many of them can be enjoyed by whatever breed you own or even adapted to suit you and your pal.

Let's start off with this game of instinct for Terriers or Retrievers, who absolutely adore digging. In this game, it isn't necessary to wrap the treat or bone in anything or to put it inside a box to keep it clean.

Try secretly hiding treats in fallen logs or under tree trunks when you are out on a walk and encourage your dog to dig them out. You can also ask a friend to walk away with your dog while you lay a trail of treats on the ground. If he has a favourite toy, try hiding it in the long grass for him find it.

It's also possible to play a variation of this game indoors. Simply fill a laundry basket or box with a collection of old clothes, towels and scrunched-up newspapers, then hide a variety of treats at the bottom. Encourage your dog to get into the box and dig around for the treats. Fun is guaranteed when all the clothes, towels and papers come flying out of the box as he digs deep for his treasure!

Although this is a great game for Terriers and Retrievers, you can make it a regular activity, whatever the breed of your dog.

Or try this: Alternatively, try burying a bone right at the very bottom of a pile of sand. Use your hands to give a good, thick covering of sand over the bone; really pile it up. Remember that this game should not be too easy for your dog.

Can He Dig It?

Yes, he can!

You'll also need: treat or bone (preferably a fresh one), favourite toy (optional), laundry basked or box, old clothes, towels, newspaper

You'll also need: a large cardboard box, old paper, toilet roll tubes, treats, a whistle

Pooch Puzzles

More mental agility

This game is particularly good for breeds such as the intelligent Border Collie, who will work out the puzzle, but not too soon, hopefully!

Place two or three treats in a large cardboard box, then screw up some of the paper and cover them up. Keep doing this until the box is full (you can throw in some used toilet roll tubes and empty plastic bottles if you want). You should end up with a box of 'hidden' treats, which you are now going to ask your dog to find.

Place the box in the middle of the room (or garden) and call your dog. Once he has scented the treats, he has to figure out how to get them. There really is no need to show him as the objective of the game is to make him work it out for himself.

Make him wait until you blow the whistle before he starts and praise him when he finds his treats. Try to keep the box upright; spilling the contents all over the floor is simply cheating.

Or try this: There are also some superb puzzle toys, which you can buy from pet stores or from the Internet. These are often made of a wooden square with smaller wooden squares inside, which can be moved up and down and from side to side. The treats can be hidden underneath certain squares. If your dog shows a real interest in puzzle activities, you may wish to buy one of these for him.

You'll also need: various treats (try to include some cooked meat as a real incentive), buckets (optional)

The Big Food Chase

Hunt for your dinner!

This is a good game for all dogs, but a Hound's hunting and scenting ability will really shine.

Clear the area of distractions, but try to leave a few 'decoys' around, such as a couple of empty buckets to throw the treats into, and create a few obstacles that can be used as hiding places.

This game is easy for you: just ask your dog to sit and get his attention by holding a treat in your raised hand. He should be facing you with his back to the garden or yard. Now throw his treats around the place, starting off with one and letting him find it, then increase the pace, so that he is constantly seeking his next treat or reward.

Try to throw some of the treats inside the buckets and behind things, so that he has to use his nose to find what he wants. Praise him well when he finds a treat and allow him to eat it straight away.

Or try this: Try this game on your walks, too. Find a quiet space in a park and play the game, using trees, rocks and gates as obstacles that your dog must go round or jump over in order to hunt the rewards. If you have time, make this a game where he literally has to hunt for some of his dinner!

You'll also need: a laundry basket, a sock, treats, a whistle

Sniff-a-Sock!

The scent game for dogs

This is a good game for dogs who like to 'scent', such as Bloodhounds, Basset Hounds and most other Hound breeds and Gundogs, who enjoy retrieving.

To play, get an old sock and rub it with a treat to transfer the scent to the sock. You can use your own scent if you prefer: just rub your hands all over the sock. Alternatively, hide a treat inside the sock and then roll it up. You need to bury the sock inside your laundry basket, making sure it's about halfway down and is well covered by other clothes (not your best ones!).

Let your dog smell your hand to get the scent, then blow your whistle and give a command, such as 'Find' or 'Sock'. At first, he may wonder what is going on, but encourage him to get involved and interested. If he is struggling, walk towards the laundry basket and use the command again, which will bring him closer to where he needs to be.

Try not to help too much with this game; most dogs will soon pick up the scent and follow their noses to the right place. When he gets near or right up to the basket, let him know he is in the right place and use lots of encouragement until he retrieves his sock. Call him back to you and reward him with a treat when he gives you the sock. Play this game a few times and vary the places where you put the basket.

Or try this: Your dog can pick you out on scent alone amongst a huge crowd, so teach him to find items with just your scent on such as a handkerchief or T-shirt.

58

You need to find an area with a slow-flowing stream or a safe pond. It's a good idea to introduce your dog to the water by letting him paddle and splash around in an area of shallow water at the edge of the stream or pond.

Once he is used to the water (and this won't take long – maybe a few minutes), ask a friend to cross to the other side with a handful of treats. If you have a whistle, use it now to tell your dog that the game is about to start.

Your friend can call your dog over; alternatively, you can throw his toy into the water and ask him to fetch it. If the stretch of water is narrow, try throwing the toy right across to your friend, so your dog has to swim straight to the other side. Once there, your friend should reward him and then throw the toy straight back to you. Once the game is over, towel your dog dry.

This is a perfect game for Gundogs, such as Spaniels and Retrievers. Swimming exercises different muscles from those used in walking, so it's a really good way to keep your dog in peak physical condition.

Or try this: If you don't have access to a pond or stream, fill a deep paddling pool in your garden and let your dog splash around and play with his toys in it.

Water Babies

Pond play for dogs

You'll also need: a waterproof toy that will float, treats, a whistle (optional), a towel

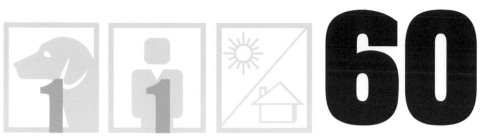
You'll also need: a treat ball (available from pet stores), treats

Toys for Toys!

Mental agility for small dogs

If you own a Toy dog, such as a Pug or a Yorkshire Terrier, there are some gentle games that will appeal to its inherent inquisitive nature.

A perfect game is to use a treat ball, which holds whatever small treats you place inside. As your dog pushes the ball or bites it, the treats will fall out onto the floor. You should be careful which treats you put inside – use healthy ones, if possible.

The size of the treat depends on the diameter of the hole in the treat ball, which are available in various sizes. The 5–7 cm (2–3 in) sizes work best for smaller dogs, and will keep them occupied for ages.

Another good way to use the treat ball is as part of a small agility course, which Toy dogs adore, and it makes them work that little bit harder for their treat. Make the ball bounce off objects or roll it into a box or even a tunnel.

If you don't have a treat ball, use a small plastic food container or a box, and make a hole in one side that is big enough for the treats to roll out when the dog pushes it and moves it around.

Or try this: As Toy breeds are notoriously agile, you can use a bigger ball, if you wish, and enjoy watching your dog wrestle with something larger than himself in order to gain his reward.

61

You'll also need: a couple of different balls, a catapult (optional), treats, water

Speed Demons

Time to beat the clock

This race-and-retrieve game is perfect for lots of breeds: Hounds, because they are built for speed, and Whippets, Greyhounds, Salukis, Afghans and Retrievers, because they love to retrieve. The key to the game is to use two distinctly different balls.

Before you start, give the balls a scent, maybe by rubbing them with a treat to make them smell good. Let your dog sniff them and get accustomed to their scent.

Find a suitable open space, preferably one that is quiet. At first, send the ball only a small distance (if you haven't got a catapult, just throw it). Send your dog to retrieve the ball, and as soon as he finds it recall him immediately. The aim is to get him to run as fast as he can, pick up the ball and run flat out straight back to you. Reward his return with a treat. Now you can launch the second ball, but make this one go farther and repeat the run, retrieve, run, treat pattern.

Remember that this is a fast and furious game, so make sure you have plenty of water with you and limit it to 15-minutes at the most to avoid over-heating or even boredom!

Or try this: Invite your friends with long-legged dogs to join in and have race-offs in the park.

You'll also need: grocery bags, lightweight items to put in them, a small cushion, a collar and lead, treats

What a Carry-On!

Give your dog a working workout

The Working and Pastoral groups of dog contain some of the largest breeds, and as their name suggests, their ancestors were all working dogs. Not ones for circus routines, these dogs nevertheless thrive on obedience and love to help around the house. This game helps them to do just that.

You need to make a pack that your dog can carry for you. Fill two plastic or thick brown paper grocery bags with an even weight of light-weight items, no more than 1 kg (2 lb) in each bag; and don't forget to include a treat or two in each as well. Use a strong piece of string to tie the handles together, so that they will eventually hang over your dog's back and down each side. Now place a soft cushion on your dog's back and hang the bags over the top. Use encouraging words and a treat, if necessary, and stop immediately if your dog looks uncomfortable. Get him used to being led around like this. After a few minutes, remove the packs and treat him.

This game will appeal to any working dog's instinct of carrying and helping, which they love to do. It's also useful if you are going on a picnic or down to the shops for a few items – your dog will be the envy of all your neighbours. Remember, always make sure your dog is comfortable while carrying things for you. A good idea, as help around the house, is to fill the carriers with light clothes and ask him to take them to the washer for you; make it a regular task and reward him when he carries it well.

Or try this: Why not let your dog carry useful things in his mouth? If you are taking the shopping out of the car and into the house, let him carry non-food items, such as newspapers (as long as they're not too heavy). Give them to him to hold and ask him to follow you into the house. If he is good at the 'Drop' command, he may come in very useful on shopping days.

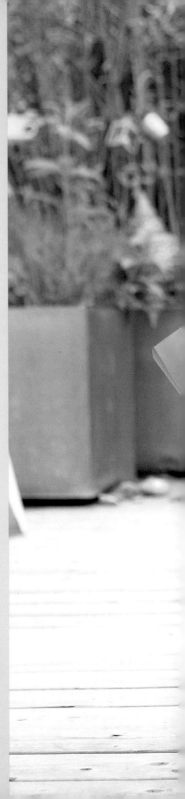

Agile Terriers, nippy Toys, and many other breeds will love this game of chase, where the target just keeps on moving!

Attach the chew firmly to the rope. It's a good idea to start this game with your dog wearing a collar so a friend can hold onto him until you are ready. Throw the chew as far as you can on its rope and then release your dog. The aim of the game is to let him get almost to the chew, at which point you pull the rope, so snatch his 'prey' back, and then throw it again in another direction. Do this a few times and try your best not to let him catch it.

Now ask your friend to hold the dog while you run off into the distance with the rope. Blow the whistle as you run to tell your friend to release the dog. Adjust the speed according to the breed and ensure you let the dog catch the toy and have a play or a chew now and again – this will also give you a chance to catch your breath.

Use your common sense with this game: don't overtire your dog and don't allow him to become frustrated if he can't catch the treat. If children want

to join in, make sure they know the rules of the game before they begin.

Or try this: Swing the rope around you, keeping it as low to the ground as possible, for your dog to chase.

Treat Tricker

Chase the chew

You'll also need: a large chew (preferably a tough one) or chew toy, a piece of soft rope 3–5 m (10–15 ft) long, a collar, a whistle

You'll also need: a specially designed tug toy, treats

Tug-of-War

And the winner is...?

This is an enjoyable game to play with larger dog breeds. Make sure there is room for you and your dog to move about and no obstacles. Hold on to one end of the toy and let your dog hold the other end in his mouth. You both pull to see who gets the toy.

There is a chance that your dog might get excited and begin growling. This is normal, as the game is based on predatory behaviour. However, it is important to prevent him becoming overly excited. A low, mild growl with his tail still wagging is acceptable, but anything more warrants a break. If you are in doubt at any point, stop the game.

Never let this game get too rough and never stare into your dog's eyes when playing it as this can be seen as confrontational, especially as you are 'fighting' over something. Also, it's good if your dog knows the 'Drop' command.

While playing tug-of-war, it is OK to occasionally let your dog win. This builds his confidence and rewards him. However, the game must always end when you say, and if the dog misbehaves stop the game at once. As always, reward good behaviour with a treat.

Two dogs can play tug-of-war with one another – but only if they get along well together on a normal basis. The game should be supervised and the same rules apply. This will help to stop it getting out of hand.

Or try this: If you don't have a tug toy, try this game with a long piece of rope or even an old towel.

You'll also need: ice cubes (flavoured ones are great), chicken stock, bacon, a banana, plastic cups

Ice Ice Baby

A cool game for hot dogs

This is a good game for all breeds, although many of the smaller Utility breeds such as the Shih Tzu will really enjoy it – especially in very hot weather.

This activity is all about letting your dog have fun with the ice cubes. Try to make them in a size that won't get stuck in his throat. Use children's plastic ice-lolly makers to make giant ice cubes.

Take the ice cubes outside, one at a time or they may melt. Throw a cube for your dog and enjoy watching him try to get hold of his slippery prize.

Alternatives on this theme are to freeze chicken stock in ice-cube trays and use them for an extra-tasty treat. Or try half filling a plastic cup with water and then laying strips of raw streaky bacon in the water, so that the ends of the bacon strips are hanging over the side of the cup. Freeze and then give it to your dog; you can take the treat out of the cup or leave it in – your dog won't leave it alone until he has it! Frozen bananas are a favourite with some dogs – peel, slice and freeze them overnight for a tasty game the following day.

Or try this: Make a beefy lolly in a children's ice-lolly maker and use a long chew or a thin strip of raw hide as the lolly stick. Take your dog on a long walk and present him with his tasty iced treat on your return.

Sports
for Dogs

There are so many different activities for dogs these days that it can be hard to keep up with them. Is that Agility or Obedience? Can I dance with my dog or should I try Cani-cross? Of course, the most important consideration is to find a hobby that suits both your dog and you – a Chihuahua will never be able to pull a sled, and a Great Dane may struggle to fit through a small agility tunnel. If you are considering joining a club with your dog, try a few of the activities in this chapter first. This will give you a good idea of what is involved and you will also be able to find out whether your dog enjoys participating. Most of the activities are played at competition level, both national and international, so find one that your dog is good at and go for gold.

Dog Obedience training is not all about giving commands and pushing dogs to work hard without any enjoyment; in fact, it's quite the opposite. It is natural for a dog to work for a human and working dogs are happy and content. Clickers are advisable in Obedience training, as they reinforce your commands and the dog gets used to hearing the click as a positive sound, telling him that he is doing the right thing (see page 5).

As with most other disciplines in this section, Obedience can also be practised to competition level. To find out if you and your dog enjoy it, and try it on a small scale first. Many of the things you have already taught your dog come under the umbrella of Obedience: sit, stay, fetch and drop are all activities in which he follows a command that you give him. More advanced Obedience is taught at many clubs and can be a very enjoyable pastime for you both. At home, you can devise your own Obedience routines to keep your dog busy and active. Make them fun, so that he will want to do them and please you, but stop as soon as he starts to lose interest and get bored. Use treats to reward.

Or try this: Put him on a collar and lead, and have a treat and a clicker handy. Ask him to sit on your right-hand side, right beside you and facing forwards. As you move off slowly with your right leg, ask him to 'Walk' or 'Heel'. Use the lead to gently tug him back if he gets ahead of you or pulls to the side, and click as soon as he is walking right beside you at the same pace.

Good Boy!

Obedience for beginners

66

You'll also need: a collar and lead, a clicker, treats

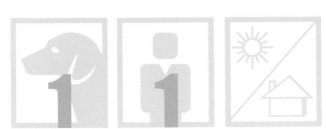

You'll also need: music, treats, a clicker, props (optional)

Dancing Dogs

Let the music play!

Heelwork to Music evolved from the set exercises forming the heelwork component of competitive Obedience, with a musical backing, but it quickly grew into a much more creative discipline. It requires some dog-training skills, and those taking part usually love other areas of dog training such as Agility or Obedience. Experience in at least a lower level of Obedience competition will help to provide a basis, although it is not essential.

A good introduction to this is simply to put on some music and start to dance. Encourage your dog to jump around with you and praise him when he does. He may get excited at first, but all you are doing here is getting him used to moving around with you to some music. Marching music is good to start off with.

Freestyle routines (where the dog doesn't have to be in the heelwork position throughout) are very popular, as they allow for more creativity. Fun moves you may want to teach him include: walking on his back legs, creeping, jumping through hoops or outstretched arms, weaving through your legs, rollovers, high-fives, playing dead and reversing around you. Teaching lots of these moves only requires treats and patience, but some are more complicated, such as reversing around the handler.

Or try this: Attend an event or training workshop to find out what's involved. There are also books and videos available to help you get started.

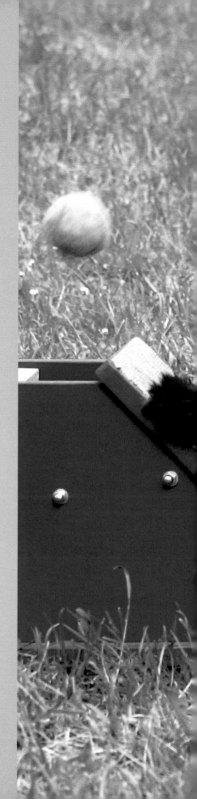

You'll also need: two tennis balls, small jumps, treats

Fly With Me

Take a look at Flyball

Flyball is played with two teams of dogs (four dogs per team is ideal). The game is a race against the clock and each dog runs a course, consisting of four hurdles, with a ball box that releases a ball. Each dog is required to run back over the hurdles with the ball, with the next dog taking over, in a relay.

To help you get started, try taking two balls and stand a few metres away from your dog. Toss the first ball gently. When he catches it, give the 'Drop' command. As soon as he drops the ball, throw another one straightaway. This familiarizes him with the fast-paced action of Flyball.

A variation on this is to have two balls and toss one 2 m (6 ft) up in the air. Your dog will jump to catch it. Give the command to drop the ball, then immediately throw the next ball up in the air. The aim is to encourage him to catch balls from different directions.

The next step is to toss a ball away from your dog and when he returns with it, remove it from his mouth and toss it away again. When he races back towards you with the ball, run away. When he catches up, play tug with the ball still in his mouth (balls are a key part of Flyball and dogs must learn to love the ball and want to keep it).

Next come the jumps. Build a couple of small jumps (see pages 24–25). Place your dog on one side of a jump and then walk to the side. Call him, holding a treat or a favourite toy. After he has successfully jumped a few times, place a second jump on the ground, parallel to the first one with enough space for your dog to run up in between (larger dogs will require more space). Repeat the process, encouraging your dog to clear the first jump, and with the next stride, jump the second.

Or try this: There are dozens of Flyball teams and classes worldwide, and all of them can be found on the Internet.

You'll also need: a tunnel, jumps, a table, poles (for weaving)

Agility Antics

Ability = Agility!

Agility is fast, safe and enjoyable for you and your dog. It is designed to demonstrate the ability of a dog and his handler to work as a smoothly functioning team. The rules of Agility are quite simple. Your dog will compete a set course, which will include weaving, jumping, running, sitting on a table and running through tunnels. During the course, your dog will be timed and will also lose or gain points (or gain faults) for any mistake he makes. Likely mistakes could be missing a pole on the weave, failure to clear a jump or leaving the table before he is told to.

The best way to find out if your dog enjoys Agility is to practise the basics in a quiet outside area. Will your dog sit still on a small table while you count to 20? Is he adept at weaving through poles with minimal help from you? Is he happy jumping small obstacles and going through tunnels?

If the answer to most of these questions is 'yes', then you may well enjoy taking the sport further. A good idea is to visit your local club a couple of times, without your dog, and observe what goes on there. Talk to other owners and ask them questions; they'll be only too happy to help. Also, find out if there are Beginners' classes you could join, whether you need to buy any equipment and if you can take the family with you? There is usually a small fee to pay for these classes, but who knows, you may be looking at the next Agility World Champion!

Or try this: If you can't find a club nearby, ask some friends with dogs to join in and start your own club. Make your own rules, courses and prizes, and get together regularly to have competitions. When you all get better at it, have a mini championship between all the dogs and owners.

Dash 'N' Splash is the ideal activity if your dog is a lover of water and is suitable for all dogs of any shape or size. The idea of the game is simple: dogs jump from platforms into water that is deep enough for them to have to swim. Generally, they perform a long jump into the water after an object, such as a ball or a flying disc, has been thrown in. The aim is to retrieve the object and swim back to the platform with it.

Competitions are a real treat for spectators, with canine acrobatics the order of the day. Some handlers stand in the water while their dog flies over the top of them before landing with a huge splash just in front of their (very wet) owner. This game is now played at competition level and is very popular, particularly in the United States.

To try this out, find a suitable pond or stream that you can visit with your dog. The aim here is to encourage him to take a 'flying leap' after the object, rather than just trotting into the water. Try throwing the ball or disc into the water from a little way back, so that he is more likely to run at the water. His instinct then will be to jump and land in

the pond. Encourage him all the time as he goes to retrieve the object and also to bring it straight back to you. Always reward him on his return and let him rest between dashes. Once the activity is over, towel your dog dry.

Or try this: If you think your dog would enjoy Dash 'N' Splash, check on the Internet to find out if there are classes in your area.

Making a Splash!

Dash 'N' Splash for dogs

70

You'll also need: water, a ball or flying disc, treats, a towel

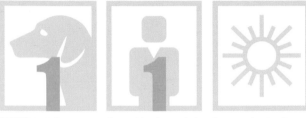

You'll also need: a smart collar and lead, a crate to take your dog to shows, brushes, a pedigree dog

What a Show Off

Dog showing is fun for both of you

Conformation shows – or breed shows – are a kind of dog show in which a judge evaluates individual pure-bred dogs on certain 'breed points' and awards placings depending on how close they are to their 'Breed Standard'.

Shows vary in difficulty, and it's best to test the water by entering a fun dog show first. These are often open to all dogs (not just pedigree ones), so you can still take part if your dog is a crossbreed. Fun dog shows have classes, such as Prettiest Dog, Most Handsome Dog and Dog Most Like His Owner.

These are also good places to meet like-minded dog lovers and many friendships have formed as a result of taking dogs to local shows.

Or try this: If you do have a pedigree dog and enjoy the 'fun' shows, check out the Internet for a list of breed shows in your area. Good luck if you progress, but always remember that no matter who wins, you always take the best dog home with you!

Try this activity to see if it's something you and your dog enjoy. Lay a line of hidden treats down while out on a walk, or even in the garden or house, to create a trail for your dog to track. Get a family member or friend to hold the dog while you run off and hide the treats, then release the dog and encourage him to sniff out the treats, which will be his rewards.

Before you sign up your canine for specialized training, be aware that it takes at least one year of twice-weekly training sessions before a dog can be evaluated and deemed fully trained. Rigorous training exercises prepare scent-tracking dogs for future missions where they may have to search for people in chaotic conditions, such as after floods or earthquakes. Above all, these dogs are trained to stay focused while trailing a scent in stressful situations.

Tracking encourages dogs to make use of their strongest asset – the ability to follow a scent trail. Tracking competitions in tracking often recreate the finding of a lost person or article in a situation where the performance of the dog can be fairly assessed. For your dog to track, he must have lots of stamina, a sound temperament and be able to work well with other dogs and people. Sporting dogs, such as Labradors and Golden Retrievers, are usually excellent at following a scent. Working and Herding breeds (German Shepherds, Newfoundlands, Bloodhounds, Dobermanns and Rottweilers) are highly motivated 'workers' and also make good scent-tracking dogs.

Or try this: If your dog seems to enjoy tracking, why not do it on a larger scale? Find an open area where it is safe to let him off the lead and make a larger 'track' for him, perhaps using a few treats initially and later, when he gets used to the idea, only one in a large area.

Tracking is Fun

Nosework for dogs

You'll also need: treats, a 'trail'

73

You'll also need: a collar and lead, CaniX line (optional), running shoes

Can He Run?

Then let's look at Cani-cross!

Cani-cross (sometimes known as CaniX) is, quite literally, running with your dog. It's a brilliant way to get out in the fresh air and spend quality time together. All you need is a collar and lead, although many owners who get really interested in the sport invest in a simple running harness for their dog, which helps with his pulling power. You can also buy a waist belt that you wear (known as a CaniX line). This is more comfortable for both you and your dog and gives you extra assistance (handy for the hills).

Get your dog accustomed to wearing a harness when you are out on walks. They soon learn the difference between their collar and their running harness – understanding that they can pull with one and not the other. The running harness directs all the pulling power to the dog's chest and shoulders away from the neck. The feel is totally different to the collar and significantly more comfortable. Running with your dog in harness can help with loose lead walking as well.

Dogs love to chase and the key is to give them something to go after. Ask a family member or friend to run up front with some treats and call enthusiastically to your dog. When you feel your dog pull, give him lots of positive encouragement.

Choose a trail that is relatively flat and narrow for your first run out, so your dog can only run in one direction, and keep the first few sessions short, so he is still pulling hard at the end of the run.

Or try this: If you wish to take this further, there are lots of Cani-cross clubs and groups, so why not join in with like-minded people and have some fun?

You'll also need: a collar and lead

Rally-O

Rally Obedience for dogs

Rally Obedience, or Rally-O, combines characteristics of sports car racing, dog agility and traditional obedience into a new fun sport.

Rally at competition level is timed and usually includes 12–20 performance stations, depending on the level of participation. It is scored by a judge who watches for a smooth performance, as well as skill in following the directions at each station.

Rally courses are designed by the judge and are different in every trial. Competitors receive a course map and can walk the course without their dogs prior to the start of the class. Judges design their courses by choosing from more than 48 stations that direct handlers and dogs on how to perform specific exercises.

Signs at each station give instructions to the dog-handler team, and each team must follow the station's task within about a metre of the sign. Once the judge gives the command 'Forward', the dog and handler complete the course on their own without further commands from the judge.

Signs instruct teams to go fast or slow, to halt (here the dog must sit at heel), to make turns and circles, to reverse direction, to do a sit-stay-recall or to follow other basic obedience exercises.

Each team has starting points from which points are deducted for faults. The team with the highest score wins. If two teams achieve the same score, the judge determines the placements according to the time recorded for each team's course completion.

Or try this: Find a local class and give it a go, especially if you have had some success with obedience activities in this book.

74

You'll also need: a flying disc, treats, water

Disc Dogs

UFO fun

In disc dog competitions, dogs and their owners (disc throwers) compete in events, such as distance catching or a choreographed freestyle catching. The sport is a celebration of the bond between handler and dog by allowing them to work together.

Under competition rules, there are short-distance events such as Toss and Fetch, MiniDistance, Throw and Catch, and Distance/Accuracy. The concept is generally the same: you have 60 seconds to make as many throws as possible on a field marked with increasingly longer distances. The distances generally don't exceed 50 m (150 ft) for the longest catches. Dogs are awarded points for catches based on the distance of the throw, with mid-air catches rating extra points (in most contests, an extra half point when the dog is completely airborne for the catch). Only one disc is used for these events.

Freestyle is a subjectively judged event, where the team consists of one person and his dog. Depending on the event, the length of a routine might vary from just a minute to three minutes. Teams are judged in categories that include Canine Athleticism, Degree of Difficulty, Showmanship and so forth. Incredible flips, hyper-fast multiple catches and spectacular vaults make freestyle a popular event with spectators, and it is regarded as the highest level of competitive accomplishment.

Or try this: As with all other sports in this chapter, try it and see! If your dog enjoyed the disc game at the beginning of this book (see pages 34–35), you can take it a stage further and join a club where you can both really polish off your skills. Competitions are held regularly, but are you and your dog up for it?

Tricks

Teaching your dog tricks is great fun and benefits both of you: it helps you to bond with your dog and keeps him mentally and physically stimulated. Whether you want to train your dog to jump a rope, dance, or say his prayers, the next few pages will show you how. Trick training can be enjoyable for all the family. Once a trick has been learned, your dog should be able to take the command from family members of all ages. Dog tricks combine Obedience, Agility and many other disciplines, so time spent teaching them is never wasted. If you have friends with dogs, you can even have a trick party, invite them round and teach tricks together, and then have a 'trick-off' at the end – you'll all love it, including the dogs.

Stand with your legs apart and hold a treat in each hand; these will be used to guide your dog through the weave. Ask him to sit or stand in front of you and make sure you have his full attention. Bend to the side and place one hand behind your leg, giving the command 'Weave'. If he follows the treat and goes between your legs, click and reward him.

Now place your other hand with the treat to the front of the same leg, urging him to walk around the outside of your leg and back to where he started.

He should now have done a full circle around one leg. Remember to use the word 'Weave'. Now encourage him to follow a treat round the outside of your other leg and to follow the next treat back between your legs. In other words, he has done a circle round your other leg in the opposite direction to the first one. Click and reward as before.

To complete this, you need to get him to perform a circle around one leg and then another circle around the other leg, like a figure eight. Practise with treats for several sessions, then see if you can do it with the clicker alone and a treat at the very end.

Or try this: Set out a weave with cones, balls or buckets. All you have to do is lay the obstacles out at 1 m (3 ft) intervals and see if your dog can weave around them.

The Leg Weave

Ins and outs

You'll also need: treats, a clicker

You'll also need: treats, a clicker

Twist and Turn

Teach your dog to twirl

The twist and turn trick is a simple one; the difficult part is teaching your dog the difference between turning one way and the other, so you need to use different words for clockwise and anti-clockwise.

Your aim is to make your dog turn in a small circle in the direction you tell him to go. Get some treats and your clicker and stand your dog on your left side. With a treat in your left hand, lure his head, so that he turns away from you, towards his left, giving the command 'Twist'. When he has turned halfway, click and praise him. Repeat this several times. When you're sure he understands what to do, use the treat to lure him all the way round, so he makes one complete turn. Repeat until he responds correctly and immediately on command.

Now you can teach the turn. This time, put your dog on your right side when you begin. Lure his nose out away from you, so that he is turning in a clockwise direction. Click while he is turning and give the command 'Turn'. Repeat several times. Eventually you just use the click and command. As ever, patience and practice are key and it may take many sessions to perfect this.

Or try this: Give the click and command from a short distance away and see if your dog can twist and turn independently. Once you have perfected twist and turn with one dog you could try it with two.

You'll also need: a home-made 'limbo' pole, treats, a clicker

Creepy-Crawly

Teach your canine to crawl

This 'trick' is based on obedience, but is lots of fun. Don't worry – it's not cruel and your dog will love learning and performing it for you.

To encourage your dog to crawl, create a home-made 'limbo' pole by placing a piece of wood on two blocks. Don't make it too low, just low enough that your dog has to crouch to crawl underneath it. The pole will help immensely, especially if your dog does not already know the down command.

Ask your dog to lie down, then drag the treat in front of his nose and under the pole, getting him to follow it on all-fours in a crawling motion. The minute he starts to do this, use your clicker once. At this point you can keep your hand over him slightly to help him stay on the ground, but always be gentle. Don't use the command 'Crawl' yet. Make sure your dog understands the action before you associate a verbal command with it. Try this exercise a few times daily over several days.

Once your dog has got used to the action, bring in the command 'Crawl' as you click. Again, it's perfectly normal to practise this over several short sessions. At this point, you may want to place the treat a short distance from his nose and drag your finger towards it, getting him to follow your finger to the treat.

Eventually, try tossing the treat and giving the command 'Crawl', and then watch how he does it on his own.

Or try this: This trick can be used to get your dog to go 'under' almost anything. Why not try teaching him to crawl under a table or chair?

Once you and your dog have mastered the leg weave (see page 120) to your satisfaction, take it one step further and try doing it to some of your favourite music.

Put on a tune with a good beat and get your dog weaving as he has been taught to do. Now you can start to add some more tricks such as encouraging him to walk under your leg as you kick it up in time to the music. You could even invest in a toy magic wand and use that to perfect your routine. You can then add little extras, such as getting your dog to go under your legs and tapping him gently on the bottom, or hold the wand low to the ground and ask him to jump over it. Use treats or the clicker (if using) each time he performs part of the routine.

This fun game is a great way for you to keep fit and is great practice if you are considering having a go at Heelwork to Music (see page 105).

Or try this: When you have worked out and perfected a short routine, ask your family and friends to watch you perform and give you marks out of ten.

Let the Music Play

Add tunes to your weaves

79

You'll also need: music, treats, a clicker (optional)

You'll also need: treats, a clicker

Singing Stars

Karaoke for canines

We've all seen dogs on television howling and singing along to their favourite TV theme tunes or songs. This 'singing' activitiy is great fun and, as long as you train your dog to only do it when asked, it can be a fabulous party piece.

There are two ways to do this. The first is to harness your dog's natural instinct to bark at certain things such as when he hears another dog or sees you get his lead. If this is the case, wait until you know he is going to bark, and as he is doing it say, 'Sing' and give him a treat. Over a period of time he will start to bark on cue. Just make sure that you are the one who decides when he does it, as you don't want your neighbours complaining.

The second way is to get your kids and some friends to have a sing-along. Put on some music and – at your cue – ask them to sing and howl. You can join in, too. If your dog even attempts to join in, use the clicker and reward him immediately.

When you think he is ready, put on some music and see if you can get your dog to sing along with his human backing vocalists.

Or try this: No music? No worries! Most dogs will pick up on certain sounds and join in anyway. If you have a musical instrument (such as a guitar, recorder or piano), try playing it and singing along. See how long it takes your dog to join in the fun.

You'll also need: a large hula-hoop, treats, a clicker, red or orange material

Ring of Fire

More fun with hoops

If you have ever dreamed of joining the circus but never had the opportunity, here's your chance. This is a great trick that you can teach your dog, and it looks just as impressive as the real thing.

If you have already taught your dog to jump through a hoop (see page 76), you're halfway there. As with the hoop game, you want to encourage him to go through a hoop, first walking while the bottom of the hoop is resting on the ground, and eventually jumping through the raised hoop.

As always, a clicker (if using), treats and encouragement are your main tools. With these as your aids, it shouldn't take more than a few sessions to get your dog to jump both ways through the hoop. Use a treat as the reward on the other side.

Get your children involved as well; ask them to jump through the low hoop and try to get the dog to follow them; turn it into a game and it will always make training easier and more fun.

Or try this: Once your dog has got the hang of this, get some red and orange material and cut it into thin strips. Tie these around the hoop and then repeat the trick – he'll really be jumping through a ring of fire.

81

It may well be one of the oldest tricks in the book, but it's always a huge hit with people if your dog offers his paw to shake hands with them. This most endearing of tricks is also a real hit with children, as it's easy to teach and dogs will often do it automatically for them.

First, get rid of any possible distractions and make sure your dog isn't hungry and doesn't need the toilet. In fact, this is a good trick to teach after a walk or a meal.

Sit on the floor in front of your dog and ask him to sit. Choose a command, such as 'Paw' or 'Shake hands'. Give the command and gently lift his paw up in your hand, hold it for a few seconds, put it back down and then click (if using), praise and reward him with a treat. As with most tricks, repetition is everything. Repeat this sequence, each time leaving it a little longer before lifting your dog's paw. He will soon get the message and lift it to meet your hand. Do this with both paws over several days.

Lastly, practise it standing in front of him, bending down to shake hands – and there you have it!

Or try this: Teach your dog to use both his paws to shake hands. Do this by holding your hand to different paws each time and he will soon get the message. This is good for his co-ordination and posture.

Pleased to Meet You

Shake hands with your dog

82

You'll also need: treats, a clicker (optional)

You'll also need: a chair, a clicker, treats

Say Your Prayers

A moment of quiet reflection

If you say your prayers at the end of the day, why not get your dog to join you? The end result is that on the command 'Say your prayers', he should automatically put his head on the chair or side of the bed, between his paws. When you say 'Amen', you release him from this position.

To get your dog into the first position (head between his paws and on the chair) encourage him to put his front paws on the chair. He must be encouraged to remain seated all the time, so, in effect, he is in a begging position, with his bottom on the floor and his feet on the chair. Remember that this may feel strange for him to start with, so be gentle and use lots of encouragement.

Now use a treat to lure your dog's head between his paws. As soon as his head lowers, click and treat. Practise several times, gradually lengthening the time between the click and the reward. As the dog lowers his head introduce the words 'Prayer time'. After a few seconds, release him with the verbal command of 'Amen'. Praise and reward him.

If your dog won't freely put his front paws on the chair, stand behind him and place them on the chair for him, then guide his nose between his paws with the treat.

Or try this: This is a lovely activity if young children get involved. Once you have trained your dog to do this, he can join in with the children's prayers at bedtime.

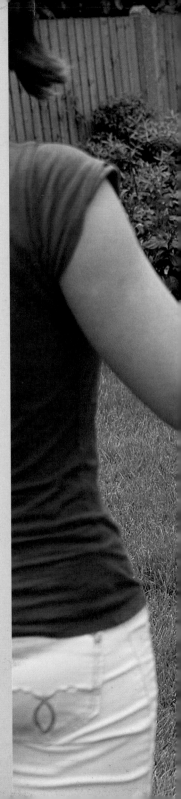

You'll also need: a clicker, treats

Wave Goodbye

Another clever paw trick

First, decide what you want your command to be. You could use a simple 'Wave' or even the greeting 'Hi!'. Kneel in front of your dog and hold out your hand as if you just want him to shake hands (see page 128). Raise your hand higher and higher each time, until you are holding your hand vertically and your dog is only touching his paw to your hand, almost like a high-five but no longer has it completely in your hand.

As the dog reaches up to touch your hand, click and treat. Repeat several times and gradually delay the click until your dog raises his paw then lowers it again. Eventually your dog will raise his paw, lower it and raise it again in a wave and you can then introduce the command 'Wave'. Slowly move farther away from your dog and click and treat every time he performs the trick correctly.

Or try this: Ask your dog to say 'Yes'. Move a treat up and down in front of your dog's nose, so that his head goes up and down. Use the command 'Yes' each time you do it. He will soon learn that this command is a sign for him to nod...for a treat.

Training your dog to go to his bed or a mat and stay there is actually more than just a trick; it is a valuable lesson for other situations you might find yourself in.

'Bed' means go to his bed and lie down and you should eventually only need to use the command 'Bed'. First, place a bed, blanket or towel about 2–3 m (6–10 ft) away from you. With your dog beside you, throw a treat onto his bed, say 'Bed' and walk over to his bed so that he can get the treat. Encourage your dog to lie down, and praise him. Repeat several times.

When you are ready, try throwing a treat and sending your dog to bed by himself. At first, make sure that a family member or friend is waiting at the bed with a treat. Later, your dog will do it himself and you should go over to him while he is lying down and reward him.

This trick requires repetition, but once mastered your dog will always respond to it on command. He will soon start to figure out that going and lying down on his bed will gain him a reward. Once he knows what the command means, try to use it in relation to wherever he sleeps.

Or try this: You can use this as a way of asking your dog to settle down if he is getting a little too excited, for example when visitors arrive.

Go to Bed

Zzzz time for your dog

You'll also need: your dog's own bed, a blanket or towel, treats

You'll also need: a clicker, treats

Say 'Please'

Manners cost nothing!

This is sometimes known as the begging trick, although it is also a good way to get your dog to say 'Please'. In this activity, you are asking him to sit up on his back legs and hold up both paws in exchange for a reward.

First, use a command that he already knows such as 'Sit'. Once he is sitting, stand in front of him with a treat and your clicker. Raise the treat in the air above your dog's head so that he has to raise his front legs off the ground in order to get it. Any move towards lifting his front legs should be rewarded with a click and treat.

Now wait a little longer each time before giving the treat, but be careful not to let your dog fall over on his back. You are helping him to develop his balance, so be thoughtful. Gradually introduce the command 'Please'.

Repeat this over a period of time until the command 'Please' sees him sit in an upright position with both front paws off the ground. Be patient and do not reward any movements other than the ones you wish him to perform.

Or try this: You can now get your dog to use his manners in a range of everyday situations such as when he wants his dinner or a walk.

This trick is based on your dog self-rewarding, as by closing the door he will get a treat. Once he's master this, he can then learn to open it again.

You can teach your dog to close a door by first teaching him to touch a target such as a plastic lid. Simply hold the lid out in front of his face and when he goes to investigate it and touches it with his nose, click and treat. When he has done this several times, attach the lid to the door with blue tac and this time when the dog touches the target with his nose give the command 'push' then click and reward as he does so. Practise several times and gradually delay the click until the dog has closed the door with his nose. As your dog begins to understand the trick and is regularly shutting the door, you can introduce the command 'close it' or 'shut it'.

If the door doesn't quite close during this game, try moving the lid a little higher up the door, as the secret is in the dog using his weight against or away from the door. He needs to get in a position where he has to get his paws up on the door to push it.

Or try this: As well as teaching your dog to shut the door he can also learn to open it. If a door is on a catch, ask him to open it using the same method. Say the command 'Open the door' to teach him to push it open with his nose.

Shut that Door

A trick for security-conscious dogs

You'll also need: a clicker, treats, blue tac

You'll also need: a large skipping rope, treats

Kangaroo Dog

Teach your dog to skip

Teaching your dog to skip is really good fun. Most dogs will automatically jump over things that are in their way and this trick is based on that simple fact. It may be a little hit-and-miss at first, but with patience and practice you will get there in the end.

Start off with two people holding a skipping rope. Keep the rope fairly loose and stand about 1.5 m (4 ft) apart. Make sure that your dog is in a calm mood and get rid of anything that may distract him such as toys or sticks.

Ask him to sit between you and your friend, facing the skipping rope. The secret here is to start slowly and get him used to the rope. Swing the rope in a circle once and see if he will step over it, if he does, praise and treat. This should be repeated several times.

As he gets more confident and begins to anticipate the rope coming towards him, up the pace slightly and encourage him to jump over the rope as it touches the ground underneath him. Again, use praise and a treat each time to encourage him. You can now move up a gear and swing the rope a little off the ground, so that he has to actually jump

to get over it. Keep these sessions short, especially in hot weather.

Or try this: Get the children involved; have skipping competitions and see who can do the most skips without stopping the rope. Don't forget to let the dog have a go, too.

Skater Pooch

Skating tricks for your dog

The aim of this advanced trick is to get your dog to ride a skateboard, but he can also just have fun playing with it. To get him to balance on the skateboard will take lots of patience and should not be attempted with large dogs. Never force a dog to use a skateboard if he doesn't like it.

Introduce your dog to the skateboard. Encourage him to sniff it while you turn it over, showing him the different parts. Spin the wheels and then place it on the ground and push it, so that he sees the entire board move. Put a treat on the skateboard and encourage your dog to take it.

Steady the skateboard with one foot or hand and use a treat to encourage your dog to step on it. Click and reward if he puts a paw on the board. Gradually introduce the word 'on it' and delay the click until he puts two paws on the board. Throw a treat so your dog has to get off and fetch it, then repeat. When the dog is happy to put both feet on the board take your foot or hand away and allow some movement. Click and reward if the dog's feet remain on the board. Gradually introduce the word 'Skate' as your dog moves the board.

A really advanced trick is to get him to use his back paw to push himself along. He will need your help with this and must feel secure with just three paws on the board. Don't worry if you don't get to this stage; just let him have a ride with you when the mood takes him.

Or try this: If you have a small dog and he enjoys his rides on wheels, invest in a basket for your bike in which he can sit while you take a ride.

89

More Fun with Fido

So you've done some of the tricks and, hopefully, you now have a well-trained, fit and happy dog. In this chapter, we are going to concentrate on having fun. From dressing up to cooking tasty treats, these are all activities that you and your family can enjoy with your 'best friend' time and time again.

You'll also need: various treats, fancy dress (optional), music, water

It's Party Time

Have a pooch get-together

We all love a party and we all love our dogs, so throw a pooch party and combine the two. It's a great opportunity for puppies and young dogs to socialize with other canines and humans.

Make or buy some invitations and send them to your dog's friends (and their human owners). You can ask them to wear fancy dress – make this optional as some people may be put off if they have nothing for them or their dogs to wear. If you like the idea of fancy dress, think of a theme, such as the Wild West, Scooby Doo or a favourite film.

Before the party, prepare some delicious treats (dog and human), and set them out in bowls. The dogs could have pigs' ears, cooked sausages or doggy chocolates.

Plan some games for the dogs. You could opt for a couple of your tried-and-tested ones, such as ball throwing (fastest retrieve gets a prize) or mini-agility for any of those who want to take part. Let the dogs play together – assuming they all get on well – but make sure they are supervised at all times. Designate a food time when the dogs can enjoy their own treats, and make sure there is fresh drinking water available all the time.

Try to reserve an area for the human guests (including children), so they have somewhere 'dog-free' to hang out and munch on some tasty party food.

Or try this: If it is sunny, why not have a barbecue? Grill some of the cheaper cuts of meat for the dogs and cool it thoroughly before offering it to them.

Tempt your dog's taste buds with these delicious canine cookies.

Preheat the oven to 200°C (400°F), Gas Mark 6.

Mix the water, oil, eggs, peanut butter, banana and vanilla with a wire whisk. Add the flours, cornmeal and oats. Combine with a mixer.

Take one-third of the mixture and place it on a floured surface. Lightly flour the top of the dough. Gently knead, adding more flour as necessary to form a pliable dough (this will require a substantial amount of flour). Roll it out until it is about 1 cm (½ in) thick and cut out some shapes, using cookie cutters. Repeat until all the dough is used up.

Place the shapes on an ungreased baking sheet. Bake in the preheated oven for 20–25 minutes until golden brown. Leave in the oven for 20 minutes after turning it off to crisp up the cookies. Allow to cool and then store in an airtight container.

Or try this: Omit the vanilla, if wished, and substitute cod liver oil for the olive oil – it's very good for dogs.

Barking Banana Cookies

Canine cookery class

You'll also need: 350 ml (12 fl oz) water, 100 ml (3½ fl oz) olive oil, 2 medium eggs, 45 g (1¾ oz) creamy peanut butter (sugar-free), 2 mashed bananas, dash of vanilla essence, 225 g (8 oz) mixed whole-wheat and white flour, 50 g (2 oz) cornmeal, 50 g (2 oz) rolled oats

You'll also need: 6 slices cooked bacon (chopped finely), 4 beaten eggs, 50 ml (2 fl oz) bacon fat, 250 ml (8 fl oz) water, 50 g (2 oz) dry milk powder, 225 g (8 oz) flour, 225 g (8 oz) wheat germ, 50 g (2 oz) cornmeal

Savoury Slobbers

Yummy snacks for dogs

Preheat the oven to 180°C (350°F), Gas Mark 4.

This recipe is really easy. Mix all the ingredients together with a wooden spoon and then drop heaped tablespoonfuls of the mixture onto a greased baking sheet. You should end up with around 40 good-sized treats. You could shape the mixture into bone shapes or even mould your dog's name with dough letters.

Bake in the preheated oven for 15 minutes. Turn off the oven and leave the cookies in the oven overnight to dry out.

Or try this: Invite some friends with dogs round to tea and let them check out your gourmet cooking!

93

You'll also need: large sheets of paper (white or coloured), newspaper, safe, washable, non-toxic children's paints, sponges, saucers, towels

Da Vinci Dog

Painting with paws

This is a fun – albeit slightly messy – activity, which can turn a dull, wet day into doggie heaven.

To set up your paints, use a saucer for each colour and pour a small amount onto each one. Make sure you have some old newspapers down on the floor and place your first large sheet of paper on them.

Your dog must be in a calm frame of mind – you don't want your furniture painted. Gently sponge each of his paws with a small covering of paint. Now all he has to do is walk over the paper to create his first masterpiece.

You can try this with different colours all on one sheet or even put different colours on each of his paws; it's entirely up to you. If you have children, let them have a go with hand and feet paintings, too.

Try a few different ideas: pick up the dog's front paws and 'walk' him over the paper with paint on his back paws, try figure of eight shapes across the paper, or perhaps use your fingers to create some funky swirls.

Remember to wash you dog thoroughly afterwards.

Or try this: If you end up with a really good picture, put it in a frame and hang it by your dog's bed.

You'll also need: collar and lead (optional), hard-boiled eggs, tablespoons, a start line and a finish line, a whistle

Eggs-tra Fun

Egg-and-spoon race

This is a simple twist on the sports day favourite. Each team consists of a person and a dog, and the dog can be on or off the lead. If you have a short garden, decide on how many times you want to go back and forth in each race. If you are playing this game in a park, have the start and finish lines quite a way apart.

Each team will have an egg balanced on a spoon and the aim is to get from the start to the finish keeping the egg on the spoon. If dropped, the team must pick the egg up, put it back on the spoon, and continue with the race. The referee may decide to give 'fault-points' each time an egg is dropped, but this must be decided before the race begins.

All teams line up at the start line and the referee blows a whistle to start the race. Set off with your egg and spoon, and remember that if your dog is not on the lead, it is your responsibility to use your voice and actions to keep him running alongside you. Dogs that leave their owners may cause the team to be disqualified. Having your dog on a lead will obviously prevent this – but it is slightly less fun!

Winning dogs get to eat the peeled eggs afterwards.

Or try this: If you don't have any eggs, you can do a dog treat and spoon race. You can involve your dog in most children's sporting activities and games as long as you don't overtire him and provide plenty of water.

94

It's a lovely summer's day and you're wondering what to do to make the most of the weather. Wonder no further: plan a doggy picnic and get your friends to tag along, too!

Try to plan this activity the night before, so you can prepare the food and have time to ask your dog-owning friends if they would like to join you.

Good food to take for the dogs would include cooked sausages, cooked minced meat and some healthy treats. Remember to pack some water for them, too.

Choose where you want to go before you set off, so you can minimize the time your dog is in a car. A beach where dogs are allowed, a country park, some woods, a riverbank or even the local park are all good places. Make sure the dog has everything he needs for the journey.

When you arrive, find a quiet spot and play some ball games first. Let the dogs explore their surroundings while you set out the rug and the food. Always keep your dogs within your sight, especially if you are somewhere new. Enjoy your picnic!

Or try this: Afterwards, why not take an enjoyable, relaxing hike to burn the calories off and arrive home with a tired, but very happy, hound?

Doggy Day Out

If you go down to the woods today...

95

You'll also need: a picnic consisting of dog and human food, a rug to sit on, drinks, a water bowl and water, a collar and lead, a ball

You'll also need: a large square of trendy material, scissors, a needle and cotton (or a sewing machine)

Furry Fashion

Chill out with a bandana

Take your material and cut it into one of the following sizes: 35 cm (14 in) square for a small dog; 45 cm (18 in) square for a medium dog; 60 cm (24 in) square for a large dog; and 65 cm (26 in) square for an extra-large dog.

Fold the square in half from corner to corner and cut carefully along the diagonal line. You should be left with a triangular piece of material. Now for the tricky bit. Fold over a 1 cm (½ in) hem on any side of the material where there is not already a hem in place. Once you have done this, tack the folds down with some small pins and sew along the hems. You should now have a triangular piece of material with three good strong edges that won't fray.

Now it's time to decorate your bandana. Try to keep the decorations simple and avoid anything that can be chewed and swallowed. Bandanas also look cool with fringes, or embroidered with your dog's name, but this is only for accomplished sewers!

All that's left now is to get your dog to model his new look.

Or try this: If the weather is hot, try soaking his bandana in cold water and wrapping it around his neck. It will look fabulous and keep him cool too!

You'll also need: collar and lead, plastic cups, small plastic buckets, a large bucket full of water, treats

Fill Me Up

A wet and fast game

This is a back-and-forth game – the aim is to see who can fill their bucket with water first! Each person must have their dog on a lead. Give everyone a small plastic cup and a small bucket. Place the large bucket full of water at one end of the garden and the smaller buckets in a spaced-out line at the other end.

Each person must now race (with their dog) between the large water-filled bucket and their own smaller bucket, with the aim of filling the cup from the large bucket and running back to their own smaller one to pour the water into it.

The winners will be the first person-and-dog team to fill their bucket or the team with the most water in their bucket when the large bucket has been emptied.

To make sure that the game is fair, have a referee to keep an eye on everyone and ensure the game is played fairly.

Or try this: Give each person their own bucket full of water and an empty bucket to begin with, and see who can empty one and fill the other first! This will avoid any arguments!

Here is a great game to test your dog's mental agility, which involves hinding a tasty treat or bone inside a series of boxes.

You are going to hide a tasty treat or bone inside a series of boxes. Put the treat in the smallest box and secure it loosely with some tape. Place this box inside a slightly larger one and secure that too, repeating until all the boxes are now inside the largest box.

Now introduce your dog to the box and wait until he gets a whiff of what's inside. Then simply sit back and divide your time between watching him get into the box and the rain pattering against the windows.

Be aware that this game will require a small amount of cleaning up afterwards, but this should only be shredded cardboard, which can be brushed up fairly quickly.

Or try this: You don't necessarily have to use an edible treat for this game. You could use a favourite toy, especially if it makes a noise that your dog will be able to hear. Hide his lead for him to find and that will be his treat – going out for a walk with you.

Rainy Days...

...can be fun!

98

You'll also need: two or three boxes of different sizes, tape, treats (pigs' ears are great)

You'll also need: some chairs and a table, sheets and blankets, treats, various toys

Dog Dens

Fun under the table

This is a great activity to amuse the children and the dog all in one go. Get some chairs and set them out in a square; if you have a dining table, you could use that too. Help the children to drape the sheets and blankets over the tables and chairs to create a cosy den for everyone, then fill it with books, paper, crayons and dog toys.

Tell the children not to play rough inside, as this may cause the dog to become upset. Why not put a radio in there, so they can listen to some music?

Give the dog a long-lasting treat to take in with him; again, let the children know that they must not take it off him.

Or try this: Use the den for a game of hide-and-seek. Get the kids to hide and send the dog to look for them. Once they get used to this, you can get the kids to wrap themselves up in sheets and blankets and let the dog dig them out.

You'll also need: a large dice, a sheet of paper, treats

Dice Dogs

An obedience board game

This is a game that will test your dog's skills to the full. Make the most of any of the commands you have already taught him, and then pitch your team against friends with dogs.

On the sheet of paper write the numbers from one to six. Next to each of the six numbers write a command. Good ones are: sit, shake hands, stay, down, say please and wave. Discuss these commands with all the players first, as they may have alternative ideas.

The first team member throws the dice and asks their dog to do whichever task is represented by that number. Set a time challenge for this: for example, if you throw a one, and the action is to sit, your dog has to sit for at least 15 seconds. Don't forget to reward your dog when he does as you ask.

Work around all the players as many times as you like. If a dog has already completed a task, then that player is allowed to throw the dice again to get a new number and command.

This game can be really entertaining and it's not necessary to have a well-trained dogs, although it helps if you want to win. The aim is to have fun, so never get stressed out if your dog can't quite do it – it just means he needs some extra practice.

Or try this: Why not have a dog/human game? In this one, the dog and human both have to do the trick. For instance, if it's 'Sit', you both have to sit. Alternatively, write some human commands on the same sheet, such as 'Stand on your head' or 'Stand on one leg', making this guaranteed fun.

The Soft Touch

How to have a laid-back dog

Most dogs will love this simple massage routine. Choose a quiet part of the house or garden. Have your dog lie down and get him in a relaxed mood. Speak gently to him and don't do anything to make him want to play.

Begin at the neck. Open your hands as if you were lightly grabbing a basketball and place one hand on each side of the dog's neck. Lightly press each finger, one by one, around his neck. Repeat for a count of six.

Now move down his back. Keep your fingers moving and gently kneading his muscles as you move them down the back; remember to go slowly and firmly but keep the touch soft. Hit the spot right above the tail. Once you get to the base of his spine, use your thumbs to gently knead the spot right above his tail.

Once you've finished the tail area, move back up the length of his body. Again, splay your hands and move up his back a little lower from where you went down it. Move to his chest. Open your hands like a butterfly, with the palms pressed gently on the middle of the dog's breastbone. Knead your fingers on either side of his chest.

Finish off with the head. Slide your hands up to the top of his head and cup them around his ears. Use your thumbs and forefingers to massage the points right behind the ears. Slowly move your hands around the sides of his face, cupping them beneath his chin. End with a kiss on the top of his head, if you wish! And don't forget the treat.

Or try this: Do this with your dog's brush instead of your hands. Use exactly the same method, and you will end up with a relaxed dog with a perfect coat.

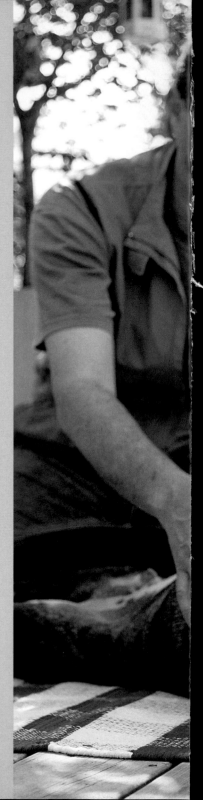

101

Index

Acknowledgements

PICTURE ACKNOWLEDGEMENTS

Special photography: © Octopus Publishing Group/Russell Sadur

Other photography: Alamy/Arco Images/C. Steimer 106; /Jim Corwin 81; /Glyn Thomas 78. **Ardea**/Jean Michel Labat 133. **BNPS** 110. **Chillpics**/Shane Wilkinson 113. **Photolibrary**/Juniors Bildarchiv 84 top right, 92.

Executive Editor: Trevor Davies
Managing Editor: Clare Churly
Executive Art Editor: Penny Stock
Designer: Ginny Zeall
Photographer Russell Sadur
Picture Library Manager: Jennifer Veall
Senior Production Controller: Amanda Mackie